Money Mind

Managing Your Money Can Be Fun

WILLIE KRUGER

HEMBURY
BOOKS

ABOUT THE AUTHOR

Willie Kruger is a two-time author and self-made millionaire who knows what it takes to transform finance from something you work for to something that works for you.

Like many people, Willie joined the workforce immediately after graduation. Soon, he had a steady job, a credit card, a comfortable flat and a new car. But what he didn't realise was that he also had a net worth of zero. He wasn't just working for his employer; he was also working for the landlord and the bank.

Lacking a financial education, Willie made poor investment choices focused on liabilities rather than assets. At 41, still with a net worth of zero, he decided to launch his own business. In less than five years, his manufacturing business employed over 100 people. Then, at 46, he started investing in properties – 15 years later, he owned 38. By creating multiple income streams in the form of rent, dividends and interest, Willie established a passive income capable of supporting his full, active life.

In *Money Mind* and *50 Tips for Home Buyers*, and through his coaching, Willie shares the simple fundamentals of building wealth and investing in your financial future. He lives in WA where he spends his free time with his grandchildren.

HEMBURY
BOOKS

First published by Hembury Books in 2026
hemburybooks.com.au
info@hemburybooks.com

Paperback ISBN 9781923765184
Ebook ISBN 9781923765191

Typeset by Lorena Susak

NATIONAL LIBRARY OF AUSTRALIA

A catalogue record for this book is available from the National Library of Australia

Dedicated to Alex

CONTENTS

INTRODUCTION

ADOPT A MONEY MIND

WHY DID YOU PICK UP THIS BOOK?

- You want to grow your net worth but you're not sure where to start.
- Will your nest egg be enough to maintain your standard of living after retirement?
- Your expenses exceed your monthly income, month after month.
- You're looking at ways to monitor profitability in your business.
- You're making money, but building wealth remains out of reach.
- After paying the accounts there's no money left for fun activities.
- You must borrow money for unexpected expenses.
- You want to brush up on your money skills.
- You're considering starting your own business.
- You want to create a source of passive income.

WHO SHOULD READ THIS BOOK?

Households, working people, and business owners can all benefit by adopting a 'money mind'. We all have to balance income and expenses every month. Perhaps you're thinking about starting your own business. Then financial skills are a must-have. Even schools and churches require effective money management.

Financial mismanagement can lead to debt, stress, and even legal issues. The compounded effect of how you think, work, and save your money every day can reap huge benefits over the long term.

WHERE DO YOU WANT THIS BOOK TO TAKE YOU?

- No more money arguments and stress.
- You want to be able to afford new cars and holidays.
- You need to get the creditors off your back.
- You need guidance to start up and build your asset portfolio.
- You need some coaching on how to save and invest.
- Retirement is looming, is your financial plan on track?
- There are so many investment options, which one is right for you?

For me personally, a financial dream come true is having enough consistent income from money-generating assets, such as dividends from stock, to pay for monthly expenses.

YOU NEED TO GET INVOLVED

Think about your money matters. Are you a spectator or player? Being a player means that you are actively involved in your financial planning. A hands-on approach will ensure that there is always enough cash for monthly expenses, annual holidays, and your retirement plan. Your effort and commitment is crucial:

- You design your own future.
- You are responsible for your own success.
- You create your own happiness.

LET'S BE HONEST: WE ALL WANT TO BE WEALTHY

Most of us work hard for our money, yet we don't all enjoy the same standard of living. Ideally, we all desire a life where we can say:

- I'm working because I enjoy work, not because I must.
- I can choose what I want to do today.
- I am debt-free.
- I have monthly earnings from passive income, not my direct labour.
- I have accumulated enough wealth to retire.

AND THEN THERE ARE THE REALITIES

If you want a healthy financial life, your motto must be: **Money is important.**

- Emotional rather than calculated spending often leads to debt issues.

- 'Looking rich' and 'being rich' are not the same thing.
- Accounts and leases restrict our freedom. I must work hard to pay the creditors.
- Financial planning will ensure that we don't cancel insurance and retirement policies.
- Every month is a balancing act, with earning on the one side and spending on the other side.
- The right mindset and money skills are the tools we need to build wealth over time – and it's all in this book.

FREEDOM STARTS WITH MAKING THE RIGHT CHOICES

*'Money **can't** buy happiness'.* Relying on physical things, like a new car, to create happiness is often short-lived. Every day, people commit to long-term loans for the sake of a happiness spike. You will never convince me that working to pay creditors is happiness. Looking rich but having zero net worth is not financial freedom. The movie *Forrest Gump* says it best: 'There's only so much money a man really needs, the rest is just for showing off.'

*'Money **can** buy happiness'.* We all know money can't buy love, friends, or time. But let's not forget, money pays the bills and debt reduces spending money. Having saved enough to retire is a form of freedom and happiness for most people. You need financial skills to create financial freedom. *Money Mind* contains all the secrets you need to grow your wealth and eventually pay for all expenses from passive income.

Monthly salaries are often used to create debt. The more we earn, the more we spend. The result is that growing a wealth portfolio often takes a back seat. Average earners often take money matters more seriously than high earners, outperforming them over the long run. Being indebted to another is a form of imprisonment. When a large portion of your disposable monthly income goes towards paying accounts and loans, your life is controlled by others. *Money Mind* will show you how to dig yourself out from under the debt mountain and become the manager of your income.

MONEY IS A FUNDAMENTAL PART OF OUR DAILY LIVES

- We need money to trade, borrow, save, invest, and compare the value of goods and services.
- It is used to store value. People save money for deferred consumption (such as in retirement).
- Interest rates are the price of money that is borrowed or saved.
- Income is earned by exchanging skills for wages or salaries. Highly skilled people earn high salaries.
- Income is determined by the demand for your skills.
- Entrepreneurs are people who organise resources to produce goods and services. Profit (money) is the main incentive that leads entrepreneurs to accept the risk of business failure.
- People tend to increase their standard of living as their skills and productivity improve.

FIVE ESSENTIALS WILL FORM THE CORNERSTONE TO BUILD WEALTH

1. Accept that personal finances are important. The right mindset about money will kickstart your financial journey.
2. You must keep the score. Make a list of what you own. Now compare that with your situation five years ago. Is your wealth growing? Numbers don't lie, and trends tell a story.
3. Good habits, routines, and a long-term plan are essential to build wealth.
4. We can all do with more money in our pocket. So, let's do it! Let's start a step-by-step process to learn and improve your money skills.
5. And the most important item... keep on reading.

LET'S UNLOCK YOUR POTENTIAL

This book explains how you can move from 'work for money' to 'money working for you'. To move from 'I owe' to 'I own'. Don't be shy to set your targets. What are your monthly expenses? How much extra do you need for those 'nice-to-haves'? Set your money goals and the plan will follow.

The good news is that money skills are easy to learn and understand. When you read it, it is almost as if you know it already. We all work hard, but do not all achieve the same financial results. Many people have little to show for a lifetime of labour. Bad habits, image, status, and lack of money skills ensure that net worth remains zero, or even in the red.

Adopting a positive mindset is the first step towards creating that self-belief that you *can* learn and apply money skills. You deserve a life free from debt and fear. All the answers you need to build your own wealth portfolio are in this book. *Money Mind* will help you to find the right combination to achieve your financial goals.

No need to do expensive courses or day seminars. Books are cheap and contain a wealth of information. You will find all these secrets to building wealth portfolio in my three books:

- ***Business Is A Lot Like Sport*** – Capitalise on skills you already have.
- ***Money Mind*** – Money is important.
- ***The Ability MBA*** – A summary of all the business skills you need.

Business books are available on the website
www.abilitybusinesscoaching.co.za

CHAPTER 1

LET'S GET STARTED

It is never too late to learn.

I started working in the building industry. The first thing I did with my salary was to buy a new car. I used my income to create debt, and I bought a depreciating asset. Poor investment decisions ensured that my net worth was in the red. Debt was holding me back financially. That was my first mistake.

While I was working, I bought land, built houses, and then sold them for a profit. You can rightfully ask me, 'What did you do with the profit?' The answer is, 'I don't know what I did with the profit'. At the end of the day, I had nothing to show for the effort, my second mistake.

At age 42 I built two houses, and for some reason decided to rent them out instead of selling them. The rent at the time was $1,600 per month. On the way to work I realised that it was more than just $1,600. In fact it was $1,600 every month for the rest of my life. I had acquired a money-generating asset!

For the first time in my life, I experienced the benefit of passive income. I became money wise. Not only did the property increase my net worth, I also had two tenants who contributed to my portfolio every month. It was like a plan that came together. Once I realised what passive income is, it inspired me to grow my portfolio and to acquire more properties.

Let's be honest, most people dream of being wealthy. Question is, what will trigger or inspire you to start your money plan? You can set your own targets:

- A monthly budget can help you to balance income and expenses.
- A financial plan can help you to, for example, to be debt-free in two years' time.
- A wealth (or long-term) plan to reap the benefits of appreciation, dividends, and compound interest.

Once you have your goals in mind, you can spend your energy on what, when, and how you will achieve your goals. Once I owned my first property it inspired me to get the next one, and the next one. Goals create focus and direction; without goals you are just drifting around financially.

Most wealthy people will admit to working long hours. I'm one of them. Having both a work and a home office allowed me to put in the extra hours and still maintain work–life balance. I could play tennis and attended all my son's rugby matches. Not all things take extra time. It takes the same time to read a novel as it does to read a business book. Cut some of the four-hour-a-day TV time. Let's get started!

WHAT IS NET WORTH?

Net worth is the result of everything you've earned and spent up to this point in time. If your net worth is zero at age 40, midway through your earning career, you need financial education. You need a plan going forward, meaning you must work towards creating a positive net worth.

Net worth is a snapshot of your current financial position. You could say your net worth is your personal balance sheet. A **positive net worth** (you own more than you owe) is an indicator of financial health, as assets are growing faster than debt.

Net worth is: What you own minus what you owe.

Assets – liabilities = net worth

The same principle applies to both a person and a corporation.

How often should you calculate your net worth? There is no set rule, but a periodic or regular calculation of your net worth will give you a clear insight into your financial progress. What would your net worth be before and after making a large purchase? Your financial life could be:

- Off track (in the red) – An indicator of poor financial discipline. You are overspending, or you may be using your income to create debt.
- A job well done (in the black) – Assets exceed liabilities, and your net worth is growing year on year.

To understand net worth, you need to separate:

- Liabilities:
    - stuff that generates interest and maintenance
    - stuff that depreciates in value
    - stuff or assets that cannot be sold.
- Assets:
    - stuff that generates income
    - stuff that grows in value
    - stuff that can be sold for a profit.

What is net income? Net income is your income after taxes and payroll deductions. It is your starting point for sensible spending and investing.

What does liquid net worth mean? Liquid net worth is the portion of your net worth that could be easily converted to cash, as opposed to an asset that would take some time to convert, such as valuable collections or property.

WHY IS NET WORTH IMPORTANT?

You cannot be sure of your precise financial situation until you know your net worth. People spend as if there is no tomorrow. And why not enjoy life now, there's still 20 or 30 years before retirement. Unfortunately, that is not always the case; a job loss, an accident, or a health setback can end or reduce earning potential in the blink of an eye. So why is net worth important?

- It is an indicator, measurement, or barometer of your wealth status.

- The trends will be a good indication of your present and future financial status.
- It measures your year-on-year financial progress. Are you wealthier or poorer than you were five years ago?
- Ideally, your net worth should be increasing year on year.
- Net worth is also an indicator of your money skills.
- There can be no estate build-up when debt repayments make it difficult to cope with monthly expenses.
- Financial stress is linked to many health and social issues.
- How much (time and money) do you need to secure retirement? If you're not consistently investing, you may not accrue enough value to support retirement. When you retire at age 65 you may still need to pay yourself for 300 months (90–65 = 25 years x 12 months = 300 months).
- Many people confuse income with net worth. Net worth isn't a reflection of how much you earn. It is what you have left over today if you had to cash everything out and paid all your obligations.

WHY SHOULD YOU CALCULATE YOUR NET WORTH?

- Zero value or decreasing year-on-year value must be a wake-up call.
- Numbers don't lie. The results force you to confront the realities of where you stand financially. Is your financial plan on track? Are the results heading in the right direction?
- What is your debt-to-income ratio? Ideally it should not be more than 30%. Are you overspending? What was the percentage two

years ago? Is debt spiralling out of control? Your long-term target should be to have zero debt.

Young people ignore net worth. They are energetic and keen to work and learn – often without a wealth plan. When you get older two things happen:

- You realise you cannot work forever.
- Middle-aged people suddenly realise their net worth is zero. Or otherwise said, they have nothing to show for all the hard work.

Where does your monthly income come from? Quite simple, really:

- While working, it's your salary, or perhaps earnings from your business.
- When you are retired, you must rely on returns generated by your savings portfolio.

Obligations such as home loan repayments and leases will reduce net monthly income.

Five things are important when we start thinking net worth:

1. *Your portfolio's earning potential.* Are you investing in money-generating assets?
2. *Being debt-free.* Own your home and get rid of debt and credit cards. Rent, accounts, and leases will reduce net income after retirement.
3. *Sustainability.* Will you be able to maintain the same standard of living 25 years after retirement?
4. *Real terms.* Will the value of your portfolio keep up with inflation?

5. *Skills.* Building wealth requires skills in earning, spending, and investing.

Retirement is not a big pile of cash that gets smaller every year. Wealth is the ability of your savings portfolio to generate a monthly passive income.

Question: How long will your savings last when you stop working? For this reason, wealth is not measured in dollars; wealth is measured in time.

If your net worth is low or you are in the red, calculating your net worth can be an intimidating experience. Take this as an opportunity to accept responsibility and to work on your skills and get financially fit. Numbers are not stagnant. You're in charge, you can change the future value of that number!

The result of poor financial planning is that many households find themselves in a financially challenging situation.

- *People often ignore debts.* Avoidance is a subconscious way to protect us from what we perceive to be a threat. If you are afraid of heights, you will tend to avoid climbing trees. Unfortunately, in the case of debt, you have to climb the tree. Negotiating with creditors, consolidating debt, and even debt forgiveness are a few of the positive avenues that are available to deal with debt.
- *You're not alone and there is no need to feel helpless.* Empower yourself by getting the best financial advice. Don't see your debt as a problem. It's a puzzle you can solve and overcome, and then you can reap the long-term benefits from your learning experience.

- *You're stuck in a spider's web of debt.* If your financial statements show your net worth is zero or negative, it is evident that:
    - you do not have a financial plan
    - you need to work on your financial skills
    - you may be spending all your hard-earned cash on interest.
    - you have no money-generating assets.
    - you are investing in liabilities, stuff that depreciates in value.
- *Is your mindset in the right place?* We limit ourselves when we say, 'I was born in the bad luck queue' or 'I never had a spare dime', 'It's too late now', and 'Do I look like Warren Buffet?' Would you rather complain than commit? If you can learn to earn, surely you can learn to spend wisely and invest.
- *Every time you sign for a lease or an account you gain a new employer.* You will work for that institution, month after month, until the debt is paid in full. Did you think the friendly salesperson across the desk is smiling because they like you? No, they like your money. Ownership documents remain with the lending institution until all debt is paid in full. Make sure that when you say, 'my house', your monthly instalments are up to date.
- *Advice is just around the corner.* How do you eliminate an error in your golf swing? You talk to a coach. If financial anxiety is weighing on you, talk to your bank or a financial adviser. Get your financial roadmap in place and stick to it. Plan A should be a monthly budget and a plan to reduce debt. Once that is done the coast is clear, it's on to plan B, a spending and investment strategy.

Pay yourself first. Also called reverse budgeting. Your monthly savings can be automatically routed from your monthly income to your savings or investment account. Paying yourself first sets psychological limits. It is as an effective plan to ensure you continue making your savings contributions month after month. There are mental benefits to seeing your balance grow and grow. Also, before spending on anything else, buy the month's groceries, fill up the tank, and pay the rent, water, and electricity. What's left over can be used to get rid of debt or for fun activities.

Nothing left over after 'pay yourself first'? Investigate your options:

- Do you really need comprehensive insurance? Accident and third party insurance is much cheaper.
- Comprehensive medical insurance often pays for services you do not use. Hospital plans help cover accounts for treatment while you are in hospital.
- Standard of living. You should have a healthy relationship between disposable income and spending habits.
- Quality of life. Luxury items measure the standard of living, but they do not necessarily define quality of life. Choose the practical; the nice-to-have always costs more.

There are three subjects that confuse most people:

1. Assets and liabilities
    - Assets generate income, for example, stock and real estate.
    - Liabilities generate expenses. People buy cars and think they are assets.
2. Saving and investing
    - Saving is for rainy days, for maintenance and education.

    - Investing is a process of acquiring assets that generate passive income.
3. Looking rich and being rich.
    - *Looking rich.* Most people confuse 'being rich' with 'looking rich.' The big car and even bigger house speak for themselves – it's a mirror of your success. To validate 'I'm rich' you should consider calculating your net worth.
    - *Being rich.* Passive income that pays for monthly expenses.

What percentage of disposable income is left over for savings after leases, accounts and the home loan are paid?

- In most cases superannuation contributions alone will not be enough to maintain the same standard of living after retirement. You may need additional savings to support your own wealth building plan.
- What about saving for rainy days (education and unexpected expenses) – is that another 5% or 10%?
- Buying a home and raising a family will allow few people to start saving before the age of 45.
- Even if you can save 50% of your income from age 45, your retirement payout will match only one-third of your last salary.
- The only exact science derived from annuity calculations is the broker's commission.
- If it seems a bit like fighting a losing battle, don't worry. Many average earners manage to build a wealth portfolio. There is a way, just keep on reading.

KEY REASONS WHY YOU NEED TO KNOW YOUR NET WORTH

Net worth is an indicator of your current financial wellbeing:

Assets (investment accounts, annuity funds and properties)
minus
Liabilities (loans, credit card debt, accounts, and loans)
= **Net worth**

Please note: Net income is not **net worth**. Income or gross income consists of salary and commissions earned, as well as interest, dividends, or rent received from investments. Gross income minus deductions for taxes and superannuation will be your net income for the month or in a tax year. Net income (or disposable income) is what we use to pay for monthly expenses and also for savings and investing. As you continue to earn and invest, your net worth will grow.

1. Reference benchmark: Your net worth is an important benchmark that measures your household's successes.

2. Track progress: Knowing your net worth makes it possible to track your financial progress. To plan, you need a point of reference.

3. Set goals: Without goals we tend to drift around in the same place, stuck in the middle. Set realistic goals. Targets that are too high have a demotivating effect, generating an attitude of 'it's not even worth trying'. Achieving goals inspires us to do better. Check your progress at least twice a year. When your net worth starts to grow, you are taking your first baby steps towards financial learning and freedom

4. For borrowing: You need a sound credit record when you apply for a loan to buy a house or a car, or to invest in a new business. Your bankers will review your financial statements, including your earnings history and your net worth.

5. Pay off debt: Credit cards accumulate compound interest against you. The average credit card interest rate exceeds 16%.

6. Mortgage debt: Consolidate all card and account debt in your home loan. Now it is much easier to calculate your net worth. A household loan is the cheapest form of debt.

7. Build assets: Own your home. Paying rent is building someone else's wealth. It's not a bad idea to own your car either. Don't trade in your car once the lease is paid off. Rather save the month's lease amount and buy your next car with cash. A car bought under a lease agreement is at the very least 30% more expensive than a cash deal. In addition, you can reap the benefits of compound interest while you save.

8. Financial security: We all want to live comfortably and not worry about money. As you get older or closer to retirement, your risk tolerance tends to decrease. Diversify your portfolio. As you age, asset allocation becomes increasingly important. Having all your eggs in one basket will increase the risk of losing everything.

Financial stability means being free of debt and being able to pay for monthly expenses. It also means you have safety nets in place to recover from unexpected expenses.

More about your net worth in Chapter 4.

CHAPTER 2

CAN YOU AFFORD IT?

Credit is one of the most powerful inventions in human history. Clever marketing strategies and easy credit facilities will make you buy, and make you pay the price – plus interest. Advertising would not be a billion-dollar industry if it didn't work. Before you sign on the dotted line, think net worth, not can you afford it?

Adopt an investor mindset when you make a purchase. For example, a cheap lounge suite may last only three or five years, while an expensive leather one may last a lifetime. Affordable cars will last as long as a luxury or performance option. No one rule works for everybody when you buy stuff.

Instant gratification has some negative connotations. It relates to making emotional decisions for the sake of instant reward. Finding the perfect balance between present and long-term benefits is an ongoing challenge. There's nothing wrong with wanting or needing products. Work on your buying skills. This will empower you to make responsible choices – especially for items that involve long-term obligations.

Retailers are experts at creating unplanned or mood driven buying:

- 'While stocks last.'
- 'Lose 10 kgs in 10 days.'
- Offers promising excessively high return on your investment.
- '50% off on all items' (except on the one you choose) gets you in the shop.

People often pay extra simply because certain items will enhance their status and image, but the value of these items often depreciate, and in addition they attract high insurance, interest, and maintenance costs.

When I say 'poor', it relates net worth (assets minus liabilities). People can still maintain a high standard of living even though their net worth may be low, or even negative. High living standards often stand squarely in the way of building a wealth portfolio that could provide passive income at a later stage.

The decision to buy is almost always based on whether you can afford it. The salesperson calculates the monthly premium, looks at your salary and 'yes, she's yours!' 'Can you afford it?' is not growing your net worth. You need to look at what the purchase will do to your net worth. For example:

A new car at	$50,000	
Registration fees	$ 2,800	
Total interest	$12,840	
= Total cost	$65,640	(numbers are rounded off)

As soon as you drive out of the showroom your newly acquired 'asset' depreciates by 20%. Assets therefore increased by $40,000 ($50,000–20%).

Your net worth just decreased by $25,650 ($40,000–$65,640). You have invested in a deprecating asset.

The bank is always the winner. Nobody can afford to save $1,000 per month, but somehow, we can afford a monthly loan payment of $1,000.

I know, we all need transport, but if we can:

- Save first (reducing the loan amount).
- Buy an affordable vehicle.

We can create space to build our net worth.

BE NET-WORTH MINDED, NOT 'CAN I AFFORD IT?'

When you are deciding to buy or not buy, you will be much better off asking, 'What will it do to my net worth?' 'Can I afford it?' is the surest way to accumulate debt and reduce your net worth.

Your new purchase looks good on the surface. Everybody can see the new car. You appear wealthier and more successful, but the debt and depreciation is hidden. Why would you enslave yourself in debt to earn admiration? Respect is always earned; it cannot be paid for.

Yes, you can afford the monthly repayments, but the signature on the dotted line transpires into long-term obligations. Don't let emotions decide; do the sums. The core business of banks is lending. The more they lend, the more money they make. Borrowing is easy these days, but the scale always balances. When you buy a depreciating asset, the bank *earns* interest and you *pay* interest. The bank is making money while your net worth is taking a plunge.

The 'how to' of growing your wealth is not a secret, it is a discipline:

1. Consider the effect of the new purchase on your net worth. Do the sums before you buy.
2. Spend within the monthly budget. Overspending in one department often means deleting or omitting another department.
3. Save before you buy (If you cannot save for it, how will you be able to afford the monthly instalments?)
4. Always give yourself a cooling-off period (at least two days for expensive purchases).
5. If are not sure, do nothing.

ADOPT A MONEY MIND

Money is all around us. Everything we own is bought with money. If money was not important, would we all spend our lives working for it? Why do we constantly think about savings and retirement? The good news is, you don't have to be a chartered accountant to be money wise. It's more about making responsible choices:

- *Be content with what you have.* Image and status often cost double, but do not offer double the value.
- *Forget about what other people do.* Keeping up with the Joneses will keep your net worth at zero.
- *Buy quality.* I bought a cheap electric kitchen knife once; it didn't last a week. Quality often lasts a lifetime.
- *Buy at the right price.* Don't be shy to offer less. You get what you negotiate. Always ask yourself: If I must sell this property the day after I buy it, will I get my money back?

- *Be net worth minded.* I'm not talking about groceries. Will the new purchase increase or decrease my net worth? For example, replacing the timber windows in your house with aluminium ones can be a costly affair, but it will probably not increase the value of the house. A buyer will still be looking at a house with windows, not caring too much whether they are timber or aluminium.
- *A budget is a point of reference.* Compare your budget with the month's spending. Know what comes in and what goes out. Where did all the cash go? If you can spend less there may be cash available to reduce accounts and leases.
- *Buy with cash.* Use a cash card instead of a credit card. It is a fact that we are inclined to use cash more carefully.
- *Think carefully before you sign on the dotted line.* 'Can I afford it?' does not consider your children's education or your retirement plan.

MONEY HAS AN EMOTIONAL SIDE

We all come from different backgrounds, and we hold different beliefs. We don't all think the same way about money. But we do have one thing in common: emotions. All people have emotions. Stress, happiness, guilt, and pride are all spending triggers. The head vs heart dragon never sleeps. It's crazy, but few people make informed decisions before spending their hard-earned cash. Even highly educated and successful people do thoughtless things with money. When we see that nice-to-have, we prefer not to do the numbers. Emotions overshadow logic.

Emotions are an important part of human behaviour. When you're feeling happy it's only natural that you want to celebrate. Shopping when you're hungry makes it more difficult to stick to the shopping list. It's easy to convince yourself you need a treat after a hard day's work.

We can all learn how to control our spending habits. Do your bit of your own 'retail therapy'. If you can identify your spending triggers you will be much more in control those 'must-have-it' impulses:

- Effective marketing strategies and clever sales talk trigger emotions.
- Sales techniques like promotions, celebrity endorsements, loyalty cards, 'only a few left', 'while stocks last', all prey on consumer emotions.
- It's only a bargain if it is something that you really need. Emotional spending is often related to shopping for things you don't really need.
- Almost everything you buy has a luxury or top-of-the-range option that triggers emotions. Think carefully before you empty your pocket for that more than you need item.
- Don't give in to sales pressure. Buy time; that's the one thing we can all afford! One way to overcome emotional decisions is to delay commitment. Negotiate a cooling-off period. 'Yes, it looks good, but give me a day or two to think about it'. Have another look at the numbers. Do your own research. Are there other options? Get a second opinion.

Empower yourself. Knowledge is power. Create a spreadsheet of your income and expenses. Now you can identify where you are overspending. How much is spent on interest? Being in control of your money is fundamental to financial and emotional wellness.

Don't get me wrong. If you can afford luxury, then why not spoil yourself? But first, spend money you have; think twice before spending money you don't have. And second, before you spend all your hard-earned cash, take a moment to consider where your wealth came from. Make sure that if you spend it all, can you make it again.

- Fashion trends, competition, and bad debt can send a business (and your income) into liquidation.
- Injury or a replacement can cut a sports career short.
- A sudden job loss means cash in the bank every month is no more.
- When stock markets crash, 20% to 50% of savings is wiped out overnight.

IT HAPPENS TO ALL OF US

No one is immune to money problems. Business failures, divorce, health issues, overspending, or a sudden job loss happen to most of us.

Studies show that financial difficulties trigger stress, depression, and reduced self-control. There is no doubt that debt can take its toll on the quality of life.

Threats of legal action and harassing phone calls from creditors often lead to debt denial:

- Underestimating how much you owe.
- Not replying to messages or not answering the phone.
- Leaving bills unopened or just stuffing them in the bottom drawer.
- Opening a new credit card when your old one is overspent.
- Telling yourself that everyone is in the same situation.

Bottling things up will only escalate the debt cycle. You need to tackle your financial situation head on to regain control of your money situation.

BE CONTENT WITH WHAT YOU HAVE

You cannot buy happiness. Being satisfied with what you have is a great stride forward in meeting the budget and having something left over for the savings plan. Here are a few suggestions on how to become more content with what you have in life:

- *Cultivate gratitude.* Are you constantly complaining about the work environment? Or are you grateful that you have a job?
- *Stop comparing yourself to others.* Your neighbour may be driving a fancy Mercedes or BMW, but you may have things that they do not.
- *Be your own leader.* When you focus your attention on what others do or have you become a follower, not a leader.
- *Take pleasure in simple things.* Walking the dog, family picnics, playing sports, socialising with friends; the list is endless. These activities are inexpensive, but the returns can be great.
- *Discipline is an asset.* Save before you buy. Instant gratification attracts interest, contract fees, and even penalties. Most people are unable to save for something, but are happy to accept the monthly instalments and long-term obligations.

HABITS CAN IMPROVE THE QUALITY OF YOUR LIFE

> *Fact: If standard of living is your number one objective, quality of life almost never improves. But if quality of life is your number one objective, standard of living invariably improves.*
> — Zig Ziglar

If stress becomes the norm we can give up, or we can course correct. There are two options at your disposal:

1. **Habits.** Adopt good habits. If bad habits can hold you back, then adopting good habits will surely have the opposite effect.
2. **Routines.** Small but consistent adjustments will produce positive results over the medium and long term. Routines remain one of the best options to improve your environment, be it personal or financial.

Quality of life is the sum of your health, happiness, and vitality, not necessarily your standard of living. Unpaid accounts or the inability to meet basic needs adds to stress and tension in households. Coaching and financial literacy are important in gaining control and making well-informed financial decisions.

The hedonic treadmill refers to the natural tendency for humans to revert to a set point of happiness after an event or major changes. Winning the lottery or buying a new car creates a happiness spike, but then we return to a baseline level of happiness sometime after the event. Rich people tend to keep on buying nice-to-have items to maintain a level of happiness. This concept helps us to understand the root of happiness. I'm not saying that it is wrong to buy nice things if you can afford it. Luxury items improve our standard of living, while good habits and routines improve quality of life.

Effective time management is how we move from busy to productive. 'There's not enough time in the day' or 'I don't know where I'll find the time' and 'I never have time for myself' are proof of being less organised. If you want to achieve your short, medium, and long-terms goals, you need to get organised. Get things done by prioritising important and urgent matters. Internet surfing, social media, and too much television will not make financial goals and dreams come true.

Time management helps to avoid procrastination, one of the biggest deterrents to getting things done. For example, forgetting to update your insurance annually will result in your risk profile being out of balance. Not adjusting for capital gains can lead to assets being under-insured, thereby increasing your risk. Not taking depreciation into account means you are overpaying the insurance company every month.

Time should be your biggest asset in your financial portfolio. Compound interest accumulates interest on interest over time.

Striking a balance between spending and saving for future needs might be harder than it sounds. I see something, I want it. My credit card helps me to exchange discipline for the nice-to-have. But do you really need it? Do your kids really need it? Put a brake on bad habits that drain your hard-earned cash. Making conscious decisions about the future is a great instrument you can use to say no for those happiness-now items you don't really need.

Nobody these days can afford to completely ignore their financial status by:

- Not knowing how much debt they really have.
- Having zero savings for emergencies, maintenance and education.
- Ignoring the need to have a financial plan for retirement.

WANTS VS NEEDS

Needs (essential items). In most cases we can make the budget work with the 'need items'. Home loan repayments (or rent), bills, health care, commuting, food, water and electricity make up our basic living expenses. Those are the items in the budget that you must pay first. Needs are those things you must have for survival.

Wants (desire items). Most people prefer not to do the budget because there is not enough room for 'want items'. I'm not saying don't buy luxury items. If you can afford it, why not? But when the purchase of a luxury item is preventing you from paying school fees or your monthly insurance premium, you are not building wealth, you are disinvesting.

In economic terms your income is a scarce resource. Allocation of that scarce resource for best use requires you to make responsible choices. Sales techniques are geared to take your hard-earned cash. Don't get caught by clever sales strategies. Persistence, limited stock and time limits are examples of pressure sales tactics. The moment you sign at the bottom of the page, you've gained a new employer. Don't give in to sales talk and sales pressure. Always say, 'give me a day or two to think it over.' Do the numbers. The performance car costs double. Can you really afford to pay double? Are the broader tyres and fancy grille really offering double the value?

You don't separate wants from needs. People find it difficult to distinguish wants and needs. They think 'need' for almost everything they buy. 'I'm a manager, therefore I need the luxury model. The expensive car is proof of my success.' That mentality keeps us down financially.

Every marketing effort can be converted into a need and a want. The marketing journey starts by promoting a product that fulfils the customer's need. Once the need is satisfied, the marketer will add features and benefits to satisfy the wants. Marketing efforts always negotiate up.

Understanding wants and needs is a core component of financial literacy.

A WEALTH PLAN STARTS WITH A SAVINGS PLAN

Savings act as a cushion to protect against financial difficulties. When unexpected expenses happen, you should not have to knock on the loan shark's door. Automate your savings. A monthly debit order puts your money in a savings account.

If you want to build wealth, you should avoid consumer debt like bank overdrafts, loans, credit cards, accounts, and leases.

Consumer debt or unproductive debt relates to expenses for items that are consumed, like food and clothes. The debt liability remains, but in most cases, people cannot even remember what the money was spent on.

Having goals makes it easier to save. Save for a deposit on a house, or perhaps your dream vacation. Don't sell your future labour for a holiday. 'Fly now, pay later' means 'Fly now, work hard later'.

Make savings a priority. Hoping there will be money left over at the end of the month for savings is proof that there is no money plan. It is very important to oversee your spending habits. Every month overspent is an opportunity lost.

TAKE OWNERSHIP OF YOUR MONEY MATTERS

Ownership = Responsibility = Accountability

'I'd rather not look at the numbers' or 'Maths is not my thing' is abdicating responsibility, flying blindfolded with your finances.

Ownership is a great motivator. A tenant will seldom share the same devotion to a garden as the owner of a house. Architects are self-motivated because they accept 'ownership' of their projects and design. Accepting ownership creates a responsible way of thinking. It's my money, I worked hard to earn it. Accountability means I have an earning/spending/saving/investing short- and long-term plan, and I stick to my plan. Ownership puts you in control of your money, rather than money (or debt) controlling you.

Building your net worth is not forbidding yourself from having fun; it's more about finding the balance between needs and things you enjoy.

HAVE A RISK MANAGEMENT PLAN

Accidents, illness, and disasters don't always happen to other people. Identify, assess, and control risks that can cause unexpected financial setbacks. When the budget is tight, try not to cancel your annuity or comprehensive insurance.

A risk management plan will protect your wealth and keep you on track to achieve your financial goals. For example, the budget for your car should include the monthly insurance premium. Insurance means you are transferring the risk to someone else.

Businesses have to deal with many risks, for example:

- *Strategic.* Competition, product decline, and reputation.

- *Compliance.* Labour laws, health and safety legislation.
- *Contractual.* Quality, penalties, delays, and disputes.
- *Financial.* Bad debt, product returns, and cash flow.
- *Operational.* Breakdowns, safety, labour actions, and embezzlement.
- *Liability.* Risks related to damage, injury, and contractual obligations.
- Other risks include accidents, disasters, political and economic risks.

It seems that most people think about risk as involving house and car insurance. A risk management plan is essential to mitigate the impact of negative events:

- *Comprehensive insurance.* Does your house insurance policy include removing building rubble in case of a fire? Are you updating your policy annually? Insurance companies apply the 'average' clause if goods are underinsured, which means you receive a proportional settlement.
- *Life policy.* Life and disability insurance is essential to protect your family in case of a tragedy. In most cases, a life policy will cover final expenses as well as living costs for those left behind.
- *Family trust.* Keep your assets out of the reach of creditors and avoid estate taxes. Trust do attract higher taxes on net income.
- *Partnerships.* 'Let's shake on it' often leads to tragedy. A few dollars spent on a well-drafted agreement by your trusted lawyer will go a long way to protecting your interests.
- *Everything is negotiable, except your health.* Your health is your personal responsibility.

- *Don't neglect your will.* If you die intestate, your assets will be divided among your surviving family according to a set formula as set out in the *Succession Act* in each state.

Risk is everywhere. External risks like wars, high interest rates, and recessions affect millions of people every year. Add disability, unemployment, and ageing and it all seems a bit too much to handle. That's why it is important to foresee and manage risk. For example, incidents can be reduced with a home security system and careful driving. A 'no claims' record will substantially reduce monthly premiums for car and home insurance.

YOU ARE RELYING ON SOMEONE ELSE TO MAKE IT HAPPEN

These days it seems that many people rely on union action for a pay increase. Some people hope for a promotion that never happens. Realise this: the union or your boss will never make you rich.

Many people experience financial crises because they have underinvested in areas with long-term benefits, such as education and training. Others invest in 'want' items, creating self-inflicted budget constraints.

It's never too late to educate yourself. Books don't cost much, and they hold a wealth of information. We can all learn business and investing skills, so invest in yourself. If you want to figure out your money problems, start off with a monthly budget and calculate your net worth. People and companies go into bankruptcy simply because they spend more than they earn.

A wealth-building mindset is the opposite of the upscale house, wanting too many things too soon, and investing in depreciating assets like boats and jewellery.

WEALTHY AND RICH ARE NOT THE SAME THING

Instant rich: An inheritance, or success in sport or music, can create an instant millionaire. Nicolas Cage, Kim Basinger and many more famous stars made millions, only to end up in bankruptcy. Lots of cash needs lots of money skills to hold it and to grow it. Building wealth will not happen in cases where 'instant rich' leads to reckless spending. There is nothing wrong with making money or being rich. But one thing is for sure: without financial and investing skills, 'rich' is often short-lived.

Look rich: Appearance can be deceptive, especially when it comes to wealth. Sprawling mansions and lavish weddings are proof of success, but often people forget to check their net worth. Rich people often have enough income to qualify for the debt they need to meet their idea of living rich. Rich people prefer image over financial security. Highflyers often find it difficult to keep up the pace. The only person you should compare yourself to is you!

Wealth: Financial security relates to the principle that you cannot work forever. How long will your income last when you stop working? Most people are afraid that they will outlive their savings, or that they will have to reduce their standard of living after retirement. Across the world people are living longer, stretching retirement funds. For that reason, the idea of creating a passive income stream is gaining popularity.

People assume that income equals wealth because in most cases, consumption (spending) increases when income increases. Even if you have a successful business that makes a lot of money, you must still find a balance between spending and building wealth. Building your wealth portfolio isn't about how much money you make, it's more about how much you can keep.

Wealth can be defined as 'sustainable and lasting' according to:

- your ability to maintain your standard of living after retirement
- the ability of your principal investment to outpace inflation
- receiving recurring income with minimal effort or active involvement.

The wealthiest person of all is the person who can lose it but make it again. People with business and investing skills often lose money, but they have the ability to learn from their mistakes, and they do it better next time round.

EARNING VS SPENDING

Let's think about skills for a second. Getting married and living happily ever after require different skills. The same goes for starting and managing a business. Making money requires earning skills, while keeping money requires money skills (living within your means) and an investing plan.

People who grow their wealth:

- spend less than they earn
- save and invest
- avoid unnecessary debt

- earn interest
- acquire money-generating assets
- have business, accounting, and financial skills.

People who struggle financially:

- spend more than they earn
- invest in liabilities (stuff that generates interest and costs)
- acquire employers (every loan, lease, and rent contract adds another employer)
- sell their future labour (buy now, pay later)
- lack money and investing skills.

We've all been there. If debt and deadlines are giving you an anxiety attack, don't despair, it is not a 'cast-in-stone' situation. You can turn things around by simply adopting a money mind. Creating a money plan and sticking to it will turn things around. Take baby steps; small successes are a great motivator:

- Start spending less that you earn, every month. If your purse is on autopilot you need to budget (also called the battle plan).
- Next step: track your expenses. Compare your actual monthly spending with the budget. Monitor and correct, it is the only way to find and root out the problem.
- Talk to your bank. Consolidate the credit card and small accounts into your mortgage account. Negotiate a lower interest rate with your bank, or move to another bank for that matter.
- Now throw away the credit card. Cash or a cash card will do just fine.
- Pump extra money into your smallest debt while continuing the minimum payments on your other loans and accounts. Once the

smallest debt is settled, you can tackle your next-smallest loan. It's called the 'snowball effect'.

- What about a side gig? Grow your income. Again, use the extra money that you make to get rid of debt.
- Adjust your lifestyle. Perhaps you can get along with less of the 'nice-to-have' or non-essential items, even if it is just for a year to get things back on track. The only way to stop paying for the past is to make room for a new way of doing things.
- Stop investing! Pay off all debt first, invest second.
- Learn to cook. Reserve eating out for special occasions.
- And don't forget to ask for a raise!

Lifestyle creep (also known as lifestyle inflation). An increase or higher income is often the trigger to spend more. The focus is on what we can afford, and eventually spending overtakes earnings. Unplanned expenses or inadequate monitoring can cause budget creep. Just like businesses, households need to manage their cash flow and find the perfect balance between what comes in and what goes out.

CAN I IMPROVE MY FINANCIAL FUTURE IF I DON'T CHANGE MY MINDSET?

Get rid of the half-truths:

- Money is not important. (If it is not important, why is everyone working to get money?)
- Rich people are dishonest. (Rich people create businesses and employment opportunities.)

- The bank says, 'I'm your partner'. (Only if you keep on paying.)
- A credit card and accounts provide for basic needs. (Debt enslaves you.)
- Buy now, pay later. (You are selling your future labour.)
- I own my house. (Only if you can keep up the monthly taxes and loan repayments.)
- Earning is important. (Spending is more important.)
- Work hard and become rich. (Work smart and become financially independent.)
- Savings are for retirement. (Savings are for rainy days.)
- Professional skills make a lot of money. (The more you earn, the more tax you pay.)
- A pension is important. (Passive income is important.)
- School education gets me a job. (Financial and business skills create jobs.)
- Most people know earning compounding interest is powerful. (The banks also know it.)
- A degree will get me a car and a house. (Salaries are used to create debt.)

Why is spending important? Good spending habits are the first step towards financial independence. Learn that:

- Spending is more important than earning. (It requires discipline to choose investing instead of spending.)
- Financial institutions rely on interest and commission (your money) to survive.
- Spending it before you earned it; you pay the price plus interest.
- Emotional spending on status and lifestyle creates liabilities – stuff that attracts more expenses like depreciation, interest, and maintenance – becoming a vicious circle of debt.

- An affordable house attracts lower repayments, insurance premiums, and property taxes. The home loan can then be paid off sooner, making it possible to pursue new investment options. Financial discipline is not a crash diet – it's a way of life.
- Spending needs planning:
    - short-term is the monthly expenses
    - medium-term is saving for holidays and school fees
    - long-term is your wealth or retirement plan.

Money is powerful. Each of us can choose to:

- Spend recklessly – you will end up working for bankers and creditors. Your money controls you.
- Spend responsibly – you can secure wealth and passive income. You control your money.

Money is power. It can be used in many ways:

- To exploit people or to care for people.
- To use bad debt for 'needs' or to create good debt for wealth.
- To control our future or be controlled.

Even more powerful than money and intelligence is our mindset.

- Fixed mindset – 'My abilities determine everything.'
- Growth mindset – 'My effort and attitude determine everything.'

What happens when you retire? Quite simply, the yield on your investment must now provide. Now ask yourself these two questions:

1. Will you be able to maintain your standard of living?
2. Will the real value of your investment keep up with inflation?

A financial plan considers your objectives and risk tolerance and will certainly contribute to your overall financial wellbeing. There is more to financial planning than just being able to pay the monthly bills.

All people have:

- *Income* (salary or passive income) on the one side, and
- *Expenses* (water, electricity, food and clothes).
- *Assets* (home, properties and stock) on the one side, and
- *Liabilities* (credit cards, accounts and car leases).

Leases and mortgages require job security. When fear of losing your job steps in, money is running your life. Liabilities make you poor, even though you may look rich. Liabilities are the sole reason why the income group is always struggling to get out of debt.

WHY ARE SOME PEOPLE WEALTHY?

- They have geese (money-generating assets) that lay golden eggs every month in the form of passive income.
- They have few or no liabilities.
- They use leverage (good debt) to create income.
- They pay for expenses and liabilities with income from assets.
- They practice financial (spending) discipline. Most important is 'save first, buy later.' Delayed rewards is a strategy used to avoid debt and contract obligations.
- They do not *own*, but *control* their assets through companies and trusts. Ownership attaches risk and estate taxes.
- They educate themselves in financial, bookkeeping, and business skills.

- Keep in mind there is a limit to what you can save. Scaling your income, business or wealth portfolio has no limits.

WHY IS THE INCOME GROUP POOR AND STRUGGLING TO GET OUT OF DEBT?

- They are the goose that must lay the golden egg (work for money).
- They incur debt (credit cards, loans) to pay for living expenses.
- They use debt (leases, mortgages) and create liabilities luxury items.
- They do not know how to use good debt (leverage) to generate income.
- They are controlled by debt, but they 'must have it now.'
- They count cars and boats as assets – things that depreciate and generate expenses are liabilities, not assets.
- They mortgage their home to the hilt, turning their greatest asset into a liability.
- They have to own. The home, the cars, and all the debt is in their name.
- Increases are important but solve no problems, because they are used to incur more debt.
- Job security with social benefits is most important.
- Keeping up with the Joneses (luxury items) is more important than making the monthly budget.
- The income group buys liabilities that generate expenses.
- The income group relies on income from their own labour.

WEALTHY PEOPLE RELY ON INCOME FROM MONEY-GENERATING ASSETS.

Expenses and liabilities are paid from assets that generate income, such as rental income from properties or dividends from stock.

Wealthy people create earning momentum, using leverage (good debt) to acquire assets that generate consistent income. Passive income pays for monthly expenses. Wealthy people rely on income from assets – income that requires minimum effort to manage and maintain. Wealthy people use other people's money (good debt) to acquire assets. Once debt is reduced, for example, the loan on a rental property is paid, the property is transformed into a money-generating asset.

Debt is a form of modern slavery. Consumption focuses on basic needs. Consumerism encourages people to buy more than they really need. Overdraft facilities, credit cards, and accounts make it easy to spend more than we earn, and even before we earn. Consumers are easy targets because they are often caught by clever sales strategies. That is why the many households are enslaved by debt.

Consider the financial situation of a household that pays 30% of monthly disposable income towards debt:

- There are 22 workdays in month. 30% of 22 is 6.6 (round it off to 7 days).
- Income earned the first seven workdays of each month goes towards paying the bank and creditors. Loans, leases, and accounts are legally enforceable undertakings to labour for the benefit of others. That is the definition of slavery – you are in essence selling a portion of your future labour. The interest rate,

administration fees, and penalties will determine the degree of exploitation.

Creditors can make your life a misery. They can seize any collateral that you pledged, including your house, business, and car. They can also force your employer to deduct amounts from your monthly salary in certain circumstances.

REDRAW FACILITY (FLEXI BONDS)

When your home is highly mortgaged, your house generates income for the bank. The mortgage on your house provides passive income for the bank, every month for 20 or up to 30 years. It is a risk-free investment for the banks, because:

- The bank holds onto the title deeds until the last cent is paid.
- Your property acts as collateral for the bond.

A redraw facility allow you to withdraw from additional funds you paid into the account (not from the standard monthly repayments). A redraw facility is a convenient way to save for emergencies. However, managing them effectively requires discipline.

Few people take time to crunch the numbers. Home loan rates may be lower than other forms of debt, but buying a car or a lounge suite and paying for it over 20 years is a questionable idea. You will be paying back almost double the purchase price over a 20-year period.

Do the numbers. Paying for the car over four years with standard vehicle financing will be cheaper. The total cost (or repayments) will add up to approximately the vehicle purchase price plus 25%.

Without exception, your home loan is the cheapest form of debt. However, if you continue to tap into available reserves, it could end up being the most expensive form of debt over the long-term.

A redraw facility is a strategy available to you. You can choose:

- *To create wealth (money working for you)*: Once the loan is paid off or nearly paid off, you can use the available funds to acquire a property to let.
- *To create a liability (working for the bank)*: If you consistently use the available funds you will never own your home.

WHEN IS ENOUGH ENOUGH?

Creating wealth has no limits. Achieving your goals creates expectations that you can make even more money, be more successful. So, what do we do? We keep on moving the goalposts. When greed steps in, new ventures are often less hands-on. We look at ways to make money, instead of ways to improve. When you only think about money, the welfare of employees become less important. We choose not to discipline our best worker for coming in late; it's difficult to be fair when money is more important.

The average PGA golfer who earns about $300,000 a year may be looking at Chris Kirk, who earns $1,000,000 a year. And Chris may be looking at Jon Rahm, who earns $6,000,000 a year. Even though we have enough, social comparison is wiring our minds to think 'enough is not enough. Greed is constantly pushing the goalposts further and further away. Greed becomes gambling, risking what we have for something we don't really need.

ADOPT GOOD HABITS

Good habits contribute to our wellbeing. It's like fastening your seatbelt when you get inside the car. Habit-forming is the process in which our behaviours become automatic. Old habits die hard, like changing to healthy eating. Still, we can choose to change bad habits for something better. Adopting good habits can certainly help increase financial security, for example:

- Daily habits can include getting seven or eight hours sleep every night, eating healthily, and getting regular exercise. What about less TV and more time for games or reading interesting articles?
- Weekly good habits can include filing invoices related to guarantees and possible tax savings.
- Monthly habits can include comparing expenses to the budget.
- Check your wealth status every six months.
- Annual habits can include updating insurance and the health check-up. High cholesterol and high blood pressure are silent killers.
- Routine care of your home, car, and the lawnmower. It will extend their useful life and reduce maintenance costs.
- Automate your savings with a monthly debit order and start reaping the benefit of compound interest. A small amount invested consistently can build wealth over time.
- Have a standard routine before any large purchase. Crunch the numbers. Are there alternatives? Is there a cooling-off period? Read the small print. Negotiate the best deal before you buy.

HOW RICH ARE YOU RIGHT NOW?

One way to grow your wealth or riches is to appreciate what you have in life. Get away from the 'grass is always greener on the other side' mentality. Forget about what others have or what they can do. Yes, I know life is tough, but take into account that most people have experienced setbacks and hardships, or may even have to deal with disabilities. You are moving around in the dark when you are:

- Concentrating on your shortcomings. You are distracting yourself from discovering your own potential.
- Constantly comparing yourself with others, wasting your energy worrying about things that you perceive to be lacking.

HURDLES ARE OFTEN SELF-IMPOSED

Self-imposed barriers hinder our progress. We place those limitations upon ourselves, often unconsciously:

- You feel like you don't know where to start.
- A new way of thinking can be somewhat threatening.
- Fixed mindset. I need more skills. What will people say if I fail?
- People often fear taking on any form of risk.
- All circumstances must be perfect before I can commit.
- Always looking at the worst-case scenario.

Lack of discipline and confidence will often reduce our chances of success. First, we need to break down those inner hurdles. Avoid excuses such as, 'I don't have enough money or experience.' Adopt a growth mindset. Say, 'I can.' Cultivate your potential. 'When I fail, I try again.

Eventually I get it right. Now I grow my confidence.'

We often think people suddenly become rich or famous. In most cases those people worked many years to realise their dreams. It takes 20 years to become an overnight success. Build your success sequentially over time, step-by-step. A house is built one brick at a time. Success is built one brick at a time.

Take baby steps. Small successes grow our confidence and before you know it the ball and chain is gone.

DO THE IMPORTANT THINGS

A full diary and a productive day are not the same thing. That's why we often feel that we met all the deadlines but did not accomplish anything. Meetings are a good example. All the great ideas and promises don't always become reality.

Unfortunately, when we've got something important to do, like updating our insurance policy, we put it off for later or simply ignore it. Distractions like social media often make it difficult to focus on the task at hand. We also tend to avoid tasks which involve making difficult choices, such as making a will.

Routines help us to be productive. Most of our daily tasks get done on autopilot. Aristotle said: 'We are what we repeatedly do. Excellence, then becomes a habit.'

Routines free up time for important things like your annual medical check-up, planning your financial future, or perhaps just spending some time with the family.

Make sure you are building on a solid foundation. We need healthy habits and routines to find that perfect work–life balance.

BE COACHABLE

Coaching is not free advice. When you hit a poor shot in golf, your partner is quick to assist with free advice. You'd be better off paying for professional advice. Lessons from your amateur friend will ensure that you keep on playing like an amateur.

Being coachable means:

- You are prepared to listen to advice.
- You can take an objective view of your abilities (strengths and weaknesses).
- You are always looking for ways to improve.
- You respond positively to constructive criticism (feedback).
- You work productively to change or get rid of bad habits.
- You are prepared to do what it takes to move up to the next level.

Reasons why you should be coachable:

- You cannot expect different results if you keep on doing the same thing.
- You certainly do not want to practise your mistakes.
- There is always room for improvement.
- Why not profit from other people's wisdom and experience?

Whether you are planning your financial future, starting a business, or simply trying get out of debt, do yourself a favour and rely on the guidance of a mentor or a coach to avoid financial and business pitfalls.

IT'S NEVER TOO LATE

Limitations are just something you put in your mind. Age, talent, skills, and experience are not barriers, they are hurdles you can jump.

Age is just a number. It's never too late to:

- acquire skills
- correct a mistake
- start your financial plan
- get out of debt
- make your marriage work
- lose weight
- start your own business
- start playing a new sport.

Learning keeps the mind stimulated. Starting something new creates excitement and opportunities to meet new people. New ideas boost self-esteem and build confidence. Charles Flint created IBM at age 61. We often tend to judge ourselves, resist change, and over-complicate matters to the point that starting a new chapter in our life loses its appeal.

The best investment and retirement plan starts today. A late start simply means more catch-up time. It's never too late to learn good financial habits. Once we created sound spending and investing habits, they become a regular part of our life.

It's never too late to become an entrepreneur:

- Employees are often forced to retire at age 65. Entrepreneurs can choose to keep on working.
- Don't waste experience gained over a lifetime. Use your skills and connections to make money. Older entrepreneurs have a much

better chance to launch a high-growth startup. A successful business is the best way to create wealth.

For most people a financial plan comprises two steps: **earn** and **save**.

A wealth plan is actually a three-step process: **earn**, **save** and **invest**.

PRACTICE CREATES POSSIBILITIES

In a business, cash flow, forecasts, role expectations, marketing, sales, and effective management all require practice. When successful business owners create a 'network', they are surrounding them themselves with support, skills, and experts that can assist with technical, bookkeeping and legal issues.

At home, the budget, relations and time management all require a level of skills. Of course you are not going to get the budget right in the first month. But we all have to ability to improve. Practice enhances your ability to innovate and be creative.

Practice creates ability and gives us wings. A bird's ability lies in its wings. It is not worried that the branch it's sitting on could break.

A job, a boss, a union, and labour laws will help you to keep your job or get an increase, but it is not ability; it is a branch you are sitting on. It will never make you rich. If you want to fly financially you need to practice your financial abilities.

CHAPTER 3

PERSONAL FINANCIAL SKILLS

Did you know that you are the owner of a small company? It's called 'The Household'. Can the household thrive financially if the owner is clueless about cash management, savings, debt, and asset management?

Managing cash flow is the single most important function for business owners. Households are no different. Do you have any beans left at the end of the month? If not, then it's time to learn how to manage your income. These days, household finance is a mini business. An honest assessment of your finances every month gives you an opportunity to become money wise, empowering you to plan your financial future.

Tracking your expenses creates transparency about your spending habits. The monthly household budget is your best estimate of income and expenses. Compare monthly inflow (income) and outflow (expenses):

- How much money is coming into your household?
- How much money is going out?

- How much money you have left?
- Deal with your debts. Ideally you should have only one debt: your home loan. Construct a plan to get rid of all other creditors, accounts, and leases. These debts attract high interest rates, commissions, and penalties.
- Take a good look at monthly repeat spending. A burger a day keeps the wealth plan away. Spending $20 on a daily takeaway will add up to over $146,000 over 20 years. I'm not saying be Ebenezer Scrooge, but the rising cost of living means that most people must find a balance between convenience and prepared meals. A penny saved is a penny earned.

START THINKING FINANCIALLY

What happens when, as adults, we are confronted with investment and financial decisions?

- Fear of the unknown causes us to steer away from independence (starting a business) and we settle for security (a steady job).
- We listen to financial advisers who themselves have never owned a business. Don't confuse financial advice with financial education. Brokers hope that you will listen to financial advice (sales talk), and that's how they secure their monthly commission. I'm not saying don't use brokers. I'm saying, listen to advice, but taking that advice must remain your choice.
- We do not know how to leverage our savings, so we hand them over to financial institutions in the hope that they will outperform inflation, and in most cases this does not happen.
- We trust brokers and financial institutions even though they do

not accept any form of risk. They will earn their commission even if your investment devalues. When you make a mistake you learn from it, but when your financial adviser makes a mistake, you pay for it.

An own business creates a real opportunity to educate yourself; to learn business, accounting, and investing skills. To learn from mistakes. To manage risk. To work, invest and grow your earnings yourself.

Success is also related to our mindset. Our thoughts, beliefs, values, and doubts will influence our choices. What will your financial status be five or 10 years from now? In his book *Why "A" Students Work For "C" Students,* Robert T. Kiyosaki describes how important your point of reference is.

A poor person will remain poor if they have limiting beliefs such as:

- I'm poor because he is rich.
- Money is not important.
- Rich people don't go to heaven.
- The rich are greedy.
- I'd rather be happy.
- The government or the union should take care of people.

A middle-income person's priorities and values will shift to entirely different values:

- I must get a good education.
- I need a highly paid job.
- I want a nice house in a nice neighbourhood.
- Job security, health insurance, and superannuation benefits are important.

This income group uses their income to invest in debt. Leases and mortgages make it possible to have it now. They indulge in luxuries, incurring debt to acquire more than they need. Credit cards and accounts create debt for daily living expenses. The result is that the middle class is constantly trying to get out of debt. They invest in university education and neglect to see the value of financial education.

Rich people shift to a growth mindset:

- I want to be rich.
- I want my own business.
- I look for opportunities, not employment.
- I want to control, rather than own.
- I work to acquire skills, not money.
- I engage in good debt (leverage) to create a money-generating asset.
- I think financial freedom, rather than job security.

How often do we see adults acting like children?

- It's not my fault. I prefer to blame others – sidestepping responsibility.
- Complaining when we do not get our way.
- Constantly comparing our status to that of others.
- Expecting life to be easy.
- Feeling jealous threatened when others achieve.

Risk and failure are not about exposing our inadequacies; they are about learning. We say, 'Yes, it is my fault'. When we fail, we try and try again. Next time we do it better. We convert setbacks into future achievements

Jobs will give us a fish a day, financial and investing skills teach us to fish.

Why do I need financial skills? Ease and convenience do not come for free. The less you know or do, the more you have to rely on the effort of others. A beggar does not work. He relies on people who work hard to put money in his hand. Yet a beggar's life is the hardest, sleeping under bridges and being exposed to the weather. In the financial world the 'easy route', the 'short cut', the 'must have it now' comes with a price tag in the form of fees, commissions, and interest.

What happens when I retire? Quite simply, the yield on your investment must provide for you. Now ask yourself these two questions:

- Will you be able to maintain your standard of living?
- Will the real value of your investment keep up with inflation?

The real value of cash-type investments will reduce in the same proportion as the current inflation rate. A 5% inflation rate will reduce the real value of both the principal investment and the earnings to almost half over a 10-year period. The question to ask is, how will you be able to retain the buying power of your savings if you live another 20 or even 30 years after retirement? The rising cost of living year on year triggers the need for a passive income source.

What is passive income? Also known as residual income, it is the Holy Grail for income-motivated people. Work once and get paid over and over again. To generate consistent income, you need to **create something that people will continue to pay for on a regular basis.** You don't have to be present to earn passive income, whereas working for a salary or commission (active income) involves trading hours for money: no work, no pay.

Even recurring income requires some form of management. There are few fully passive income sources. Properties, for example, require constant maintenance. The aim is to secure ongoing income with minimum input from you.

ADVANTAGES OF CREATING A PASSIVE INCOME

- You can augment your income while you are still working. Buying and renting out a second home takes little time.
- While working full time on your job you can work part-time on your hobby or side-hustle. A side-hustle can be a great opportunity to expand your skillset, and it may well be the seed to start and grow your own venture.
- Your income is protected should you lose your job or become incapacitated.
- You are learning business and investment skills.
- You secure recurring income when you retire.
- Creating wealth has no limits.

Why is financial education important? A financial plan considers your objectives and risk tolerance and will certainly contribute to your overall financial wellbeing. There is more to financial planning than just being able to pay the monthly bills. You should be asking yourself:

- What is my net worth now and where do I want to be in five or 10 years?
- Do I want to keep working payday to payday, or can I create my own income, money working for me?

- Am I indulging in lifestyle and status, while educated financial decisions are taking a back seat?
- Is 'keeping up with the Joneses' more important than the long-term plan?

THE MOST IMPORTANT THINGS IN PERSONAL FINANCE

Start thinking like a business owner:

- *Manage your debt.* Consolidate all debt in your mortgage. It's easier to manage a single monthly payment.
- *Have a plan to reduce debt and eventually be totally debt-free.* When debt spirals out of control there can be no wealth building.
- *Short and long-term planning.* Set realistic targets to get things going in the right direction.
- *Invest both in skills and assets.* We need skills to acquire assets, but we also need skills to manage assets.
- *Tax planning.* Take advantage of the many available tax breaks. Consider a family trust; it will protect your assets if you decide to start a business.
- *Build an emergency fund.* Set up an automatic transfer to your savings account. A bit of cash on the side offers you instant access to cover the cost of unplanned expenses like maintenance or even a job loss.
- *Risk management.* Insurance for your house, household, vehicles, and your life. Don't think about it, just pay it!
- *Retirement planning.* Retirement plans offer valuable tax breaks.
- *Build a good credit score.* The biggest expense over your lifetime

will be costs of interest on your mortgage and car loans. A solid credit score qualifies you for better interest rates, saving you tens of thousands of dollars over the long-term.

- *Build equity.* Own your home. A portion of monthly payments go towards interest, but the balance builds equity.
- *Know what comes in and how it goes* out. The author John C. Maxwell explains budgeting perfectly: 'A budget is telling your money where to go instead of wondering where it went.'
- *Cash flow management.* The four golden rules:
    1. Create a budget.
    2. Track your expenses.
    3. Reduce debt.
    4. Automate your savings.

How much cash should you have for emergency funds, holidays, maintenance and even pandemics? Personally, I never have much cash on hand. My money is always tied up in a building project or a venture. Liquid securities like stock can take care of emergencies. 'Cash is king' is more about managing cash, not keeping money under the mattress.

FINANCIAL SKILLS CAN MAKE A DIFFERENCE

Many people don't like to do the numbers, saying, 'Maths and accounting is just not my thing'. The reality is, it should be your thing. We all need money, we all work for money, and we all spend money. Ignoring spending patterns or making only minimum payments on credit cards are two common mistakes that borrowers make. Debt strains mental health, and that can lead to stressed relationships.

Taking advice from the estate agent, the car salesperson, or brokers is easy and convenient, but you are listening to sales talk. Borrowing to buy a watch or a car is easy. The reality kicks in the moment you sign – that's the point in time when you start paying interest and commission. The 'short-term easy' transpires into long-term obligations. Advice and education are not the same thing. Advice is not free; it generates income for the advisers.

Accept the fact that you need skills to navigate your financial future. The good news is that basic accounting, business and financial skills are easy to learn and understand.

Start off with getting your mindset in the right place – money is important. Think about it this way:

- It's not only about retirement, but also about security and maintaining lifestyle expectations.
- Healthy spending habits will help you to make the most of your money.

The fact is, most people know how to earn or make money, but few of us have sophisticated investing skills. Investing in bonds, mutual funds, and annuities requires less skills. Trading in currencies and stock will require you to open a brokerage account with a reputable broker.

What is investing? It is a long-term plan to create wealth.

What is wealth? It is money working for you without your direct labour.

Borrowing money to purchase, for example, a rented property, is using good debt to create passive income, every month. Once the mortgage is paid off (by the tenant), you have a money-generating asset. You converted **working for money** into **money working for you**. The mortgage liability is transferred to the tenant. Income now flows from your asset, not your own labour. The direction that your money flows (cash flow) will determine your wealth:

- Are your paying rent (liability) or are you receiving rent (asset)?
- Are you paying interest (expense) or are you receiving dividends (income)?
- Are you paying accounts from a salary (own labour) or with income from assets or business (passive income)?

STRATEGIES TO IMPROVE YOUR FINANCIAL LITERACY SKILLS

Developing financial literacy is a choice. When cash is short, annuities and insurance premiums are often the first items people cancel or default on. To grow your net worth requires learning and practice – and a bit of discipline. Managing your financial affairs will include achieving short and long-term goals:

- The monthly budget (short-term).
- Managing tax obligations, accounts, leases, and credit cards (short-term).
- Managing mortgages (long-term).
- Insurance (short-term).
- Estate planning includes your will, naming an executor, and guardianship of children and pets (long-term).
- Life, funeral, and disability cover (long-term).

- Savings and net worth (short-term).
- Investments and a retirement plan (long-term).

Be prepared to deal with those things life throws at you:

- **Banking services:** Know what banking services are available. A good credit score means that you will qualify for lower interest rates. A bad credit score brands you as a risky bet.
- **Pay bills promptly.** Stay on top of monthly bills, making sure that payments are consistently made and on time. Consider taking advantage of automatic debits from a current account.
- **Pay yourself first.** To build savings, reverse budgeting involves choosing a savings goal and deciding how much you want to contribute towards it each month.
- **Insurance.** Your car being stolen, accidents and health setbacks are things we cannot avoid. Insurance is an absolute must to avoid financial disaster, including:
    - health insurance (an accident and hospital plan is sufficient), life and disability cover.
    - car, home and household insurance (insuring for small things like rings and cameras is expensive and unnecessary).
    - key person policy for business owners.

Manage debt. Don't be a sucker for punishment. Debt enslaves you.

- Your budget is your tool to make sure that you are not spending more than your monthly income.
- Build a smart relationship with your money. Financial literacy is not a crash diet, it is a way of life. Decision-making skills will help you to weigh options and make informed choices that will align with your short and long-term financial goals.

YES, I KNOW, BOOKKEEPING IS BORING...

But this is where we count the beans. Running a household these days can be overwhelming. Most people find the balancing act between income and expenses quite challenging. One way to keep things on track is to take an accounting approach. I know your household is not really a business, but neither are schools and churches. Even these institutions can only survive when managed like a business. Now, I'm not saying you must employ a full-time accountant, but it is important to balance the income and outgoing scale.

For example, it is important to know the difference between gross and net income. Interest and expenses are paid from net income.

Each transaction creates either value or a liability. When selling its products, a business receives cash (value increase), in exchange for merchandise (value decrease). For example:

- buying a vehicle (asset increase)
- in exchange for signing a lease contract (liability increase).

Financial literacy is an asset in your bag. Understanding the financial components of budgeting, investing, borrowing, and taxation is the first step towards creating wealth and moving away from bad debt. People should not assume their kids will somehow learn about money on their own. In fact, they learn by example. Raising your kids to be smart with money is giving then a vital life skill. Tell them why you must go to work. For example, while shopping explain to them:

- why you choose on product over another
- compare price per unit or price by weight
- a set of six may offer better value
- we pay for needs first, then the 'nice-to-haves'.

Chores teach kids life skills. Negotiate paying them to do certain tasks, like mowing the lawn, taking out the rubbish, or walking the dog. Teach them how to save up for a bicycle or holiday spending money. Introduce them to opportunity cost; it's the video game or the roller skates, not both.

Household bookkeeping (it is your monthly budget) is the starting point of wealth management. You cannot grow wealth (save and invest) if there is nothing left at the of the month. If ends don't meet, you can start off with some quick fixes like cancelling subscriptions and streaming services. Make cooking fun and save on restaurants. Trade trips to the mall for walks in the park. Pack your own lunch; daily takeaway adds up. Once you know where the money goes you can tighten the reins on areas where you're overspending. Insurance premiums, home loan interest rates, and bank charges can be negotiated. And don't forget to ask for a raise! More about the budget in Chapter 4.

BOOKKEEPING IS NOT COMPLEX; IT REVOLVES AROUND ONLY TWO THINGS:

- Income vs expenses (the budget, see Chapter 4).
- Assets vs liabilities (net worth).

Assets. The value of assets tend to be dynamic, moving targets. Stock is volatile and vehicles depreciate. Even things that might seem stable, like the value of your home, will change based on current comparable market values.

There is more to managing assets than just servicing the car or painting the house. Step one is knowing and listing your assets in order of importance. Ever wondered what your greatest assets are? (It may be yourself):

- *Your physical health.* Annual check-ups put you in charge of your health. Making a doctor's appointment only when you're sick is a thing of the past. Cancer, cholesterol, diabetes, and heart conditions all require early diagnosis.
- *Your mental health.* Debt is known to cause mental health issues related to stress, depression, and anxiety.
- *Skills.* Earning on the one side and budgeting, spending, saving, investing, risk, debt, and retirement on the other side, all require a level of financial skills.

The best investment you can make, is an investment in yourself... The more you learn, the more you'll earn. – Warren Buffett

An asset is a resource owned by you and which has a future economic benefit. Assets can be converted to cash (meaning they have a cash value). Make a list of your assets. Common assets include:

- Cash and cash equivalents, for example money market funds or CDs (certificates of deposit).
- Your holiday home (it can be rented out to generate income).
- Your own business, including accounts receivable and inventory.
- Vehicles, plant, and equipment.
- Real estate and other properties (homes, land, timeshares).
- Stocks, mutual and retirement funds.
- Collectors' items such as jewellery, vehicles, art, and rare stamps.
- Trademarks, patents, and royalty agreements (intangible assets).

It takes a bit of practice to understand the value of your assets. The most valuable assets those things we cannot see. Business owners often place value on machines and equipment. Since anybody can buy machines, owners should concentrate more on the intangibles to gain a competitive edge, such as a secure customer base, brand, and patents. Your skills and ability to learn and improve should be the greatest asset in your bag.

Your car was purchased for a certain amount, but it immediately lost value (depreciated) when you drove it out of the showroom. For example, a new car costs $50,000. But once you drive out of the showroom the resale value may only be $35,000 (you acquired a depreciating asset!). If the total lease payments over four years are $65,000 your net worth just decreased by $30,000! (65 000 – 35 000 = 30 000). But since you must have a car to get to work, avoid spending more than you need to. When you rush to acquire 'assets', it is important to check the effect on your net worth before and after the purchase, making sure that debt is not compounding against you.

Liabilities. Things that reduce your spending money (disposable income). A liability is an obligation between two parties that hasn't yet been fulfilled or paid in full. Mortgages, leases, accounts, and credit cards ensure that most households struggle to make ends meet. Household debt is the sum of consumer debt (current) and mortgage loans (long-term debt):

- **Household current liabilities (consumer debt).** Revolving debt or monthly obligations include accounts, credit card balances, and rent payments. Short-term debt can also include car leases, which can be justified as we need to go to work, go shopping, and so on. Ease of obtaining debt for non-essentials like a big-screen television result in consumers accumulating debt beyond their means to repay it.

- **Long-term liabilities** (or long-term debt) includes mortgages, student loans, long-term leases, and deferred taxes.

Business liabilities are incurred by owners to run a business. Typically, they represent money owed for operating expenses, such as accounts payable, wages, and taxes. In other words, obligations that are payable within one year, but more likely within a month. Expenses not paid immediately become a liability. Assets – liabilities = owner's equity.

Make a list of all your debts. A debt is something that is owed. Common examples of debt (liabilities), include:

- loans and credit card debt
- alimony
- the amount you owe on your mortgage(s) or property
- the amount you owe on your vehicles
- credit card balances or outstanding lines of credit
- taxes
- medical bills
- debt judgments
- personal loans.

In short, assets put money in your pocket and liabilities take money out. Liabilities refer to things that you owe or have borrowed, whereas assets are things that you own or that are owed to you.

Liabilities work against your net worth. In most cases, liabilities are associated with interest, sureties, and obligations under a contract.

Increasing your assets while decreasing liabilities will grow your net worth.

Know it – manage it. List what own and what you owe.

Assets on the left, liabilities on the right. Once you have all the facts in front of you, it's much easier to understand, manage, and plan for the future.

NOBODY IS EXCLUDED FROM INFLATION

Understanding key investment risks is crucial for investors to develop effective hedging strategies to preserve wealth after retirement. The erosion of purchasing power due to inflation is a source of concern for investors who invest in stocks over long investment horizons. Investors should seek investment opportunities that retain the purchasing power of their money and that will generate a return more than inflation.

Commodities such as gold are a good option to hedge against inflation as the value of your investment portfolio is protected during times of rising inflation.

A property owner can increase monthly rent according to inflation. Property is an asset class that is highly correlated to inflation.

A diversified portfolio can outperform inflation. Real growth assets, such as equity in stock, will earn dividends and can be resold with capital gain.

Inflation does not mean you have less money. You still have the same amount of money, but inflation reduces the buying power (real value) of your money.

Example: An investment of $1,000,000 yields $50,000 a year at 5% interest. Inflation at 5% will reduce the buying power to $47,500 over one year. Economists consider moderate inflation a sign of a healthy economy. Inflation should encourage you to invest rather than store your money under the mattress. The basic formula to calculate the inflation rate is as follows:

(Current price – Former price) ÷ Former price

It is important to think in real terms – what will the buying power of my savings be in five or 10 years' time?

HOW CAN YOU HEDGE AGAINST INFLATION?

- A well-diversified stock portfolio.
- Commodities like gold are a traditional inflation hedge.
- Real Estate Investment Trusts (REITs).
- Negotiate before you buy. Beat inflation by negotiating a 10% discount.
- Start your own business. Start small; it reduces risk and gives you the opportunity to learn business skills. The return on investment (ROI) from growing a successful business from a small investment is infinite.
- Residential property is a low-risk, money-generating investment, and it offers an ideal opportunity to work with your money yourself.

INTEREST (DEBT) CAN BE GOOD OR BAD

Are you paying interest? Do you receive anything of value in return? What percentage of your income is spent on interest?

Bad debt (bad interest) is associated with high interest rates and is usually the result of a revolving line of credit where the items you purchase have little value. These purchases are seldom considered necessities. Get rid of your credit card and accounts. When we buy food and clothes using cash we tend make much better choices.

The financial sector needs interest to survive. The mortgage on your home is 'good debt', but only if you pay off the loan in 20 years or less. Redraw facilities and 30-year home loans turn 'good debt' into 'bad debt' as the lease obligation will take up the majority of your working life. Redraw facilities ensure that lenders spend their whole working careers paying interest.

Good debt (good interest) results in purchases that are considered necessities and have lower interest rates. A perfect example of good interest is a mortgage. Interest rates on mortgages are lower. When you reduce the loan amount you are building equity, eventually turning your home into an asset.

Understanding the potential of exponential growth is essential for investors looking to optimise their income and to create wealth. Before you take the investment leap, make sure that you understand these principles:

Simple interest. Most home loans use simple interest. That is, interest is calculated on the principal, or original, amount of a loan. The amount owed at the end of the lending period is known as the future value of the principal. A loan of $10,000 will accrue to $10,500 at 5% interest over 12 months.

Simple interest = P x r x t
= 10,000 x 0.05 x 1
= $500

P = principal amount
r = interest rate
t = time in years.

Compound interest. Earning 'interest on interest.' Compound interest is the interest calculated on the initial principal and the previously accumulated interest. From an investor's perspective, compound interest is 'your money working for you.' Warren Buffett's secret to success is time, not high returns. The money initially deposited is called the principal amount.

Albert Einstein called compound interest 'the eighth wonder of the world'. If you don't believe me or Albert, talk to someone whose credit card is out of control. A savings plan may be boring to start off with, but consistent savings build momentum over time.

The power of compound interest. People look at numbers and think they cannot become millionaires. Compound interest creates a snowball effect, growing your funds bigger and faster. The main factor is start early. Investing takes time, just like learning and training.

The growth rate of accumulated interest is directly related to the 'compounding periods.' Interest accrued yearly will be less than monthly compound interest.

The table below shows interest earned for $1,000 invested over a 10-year period at 5% interest. Interest compounded monthly yields a 60% return.

Year 1	$1,050	Year 6	$1,340
Year 2	$1,103	Year 7	$1,407
Year 3	$1,158	Year 8	$1,477
Year 4	$1,216	Year 9	$1,551
Year 5	$1,276	Year 10	$1,629

Compound interest can also work against you. The majority of credit cards compound interest on a daily basis. Interest paid on debt outperforms interest earned. To get ahead, use your savings to earn interest. Accounts, credit cards, and loans compound against you.

Rule 72 of compound interest. How many years will it take to double the amount invested at a given interest rate? Simple: just divide the compound interest rate by 72. For example: at 9% interest, it will take (72 ÷ 9) = 8 years to double the principal amount. Earning compound interest on a daily balance is an effective investment strategy to keep your investment ahead of inflation.

Real value. This is the nominal (or current) value adjusted for inflation.

Nominal value – the effect (or rate) of inflation = real value.

For example: $1,000 invested at 10% interest for 12 months = $1,100 nominal value.

If the rate of inflation is 6%, it means that the buying power of $1,000 will be reduced by $60 in the same period.

Inflation reduced the real value (or buying power) of my $1,000 to $940 over the 12-month period. The growth on my investment in real terms is then only $40 ($100 – $60).

Interest rates offered by financial institutions often do not outperform the rate of inflation, which means that most savings do not grow in real terms.

Time value of money. Since money is not 'free', it attaches different present and future values. Money is always earned. Either you work for money or your money works for you. For that reason, money has a price attached to it in the form of interest.

How much more will your dollar be worth in the future? It all depends on your ability to invest and grow your money. This concept is called the 'time value of money.' The future value of your dollar can be increased either by:

- investment, in which case the future value will depend on the rate of return, or
- growth, by investing in an investment portfolio, shares, or some form of business activity.

We attach value to having the money now rather than in the future. If I borrow $1,000 at 10% interest, open a hot dog stand and make

$800, I'm ahead. The price I paid, namely $100 to have the money now, enabled me to make $700 net.

In principle, a dollar received today is more valuable than a dollar received in the future. Or, conversely, a dollar received in the future is worth less than a dollar received today.

Create momentum. Once you have a little sum in the piggy bank, consider gaining momentum by investing in a managed fund or ETFs. These funds allow you to diversify you saving portfolio.

Money has a price. It's called interest. Interest applies when you borrow and when you save. Interest rates should always be at the centre of your financial decisions. Interest is the cost of borrowing money. The borrower pays interest and the lender receives it.

Most home mortgages use simple interest. However, most leases and loans use compound interest, which is applied to the principal and to the accumulated interest of previous periods.

Loans can be used to build wealth. They are an instrument available to you for the purchase of your home, or perhaps to pay for education. However, when debt is used irresponsibly, it could spiral you into a debt trap.

Bad interest often relates to poor lifestyle choices, incurring debt for consumables, image, or those 'must have it now' items.

Good interest relates to debt incurred to acquire a money-generating asset. Good interest is recorded as an expense, reducing your tax liability.

The effect of time. Day traders rely on timing. Investors rely on time. And time is the single most important ingredient in investing:

- *Time and luck.* Golfer Gary Player said, 'The more I practice, the luckier I get'. It is as true in finance as it is in golf. It's easy to be drawn to 'get rich quick' stories. Making educated investment decisions takes time. Investing in the stock market without any prior research is not much different from playing the lottery. Education, research, and practice will only happen over time.
- *Time and risk.* Time neutralises small mistakes you made along the way. Increasing your time horizon is your most powerful tool in investing. Markets trend upwards in the long run. Market risk (or volatility risk) is a larger concern for short- and medium-term investment horizons.
- *Time and returns.* Do you want to know how you can get your money to really work for you? The formula for the best returns is (time + compound interest).

Time and interest. Consider the time effect of interest. For example, the total interest due on a home loan of $1,000,000 over different mortgage periods at a 6% interest rate:

- over a mortgage period of 10 years interest adds up to $360,000
- over a mortgage period of 20 years interest adds up to $760,000
- over a mortgage period of 30 years interest adds up to $1,250,000.

Please note I rounded off the figures.

You can do these sums yourself. The interest calculators on Google are easy to use. Now, I'm not saying don't buy a house. I'm saying consider paying off your home loan as early as possible. Buying an affordable home will enable you to pay extra and reduce the mortgage period.

Extra dollars paid into the home loan will directly reduce the principal debt, since the interest is already deducted from your agreed monthly instalment. Reducing your home loan payback period to 10 years can save interest charges of ($1,250,000 – $360,000), almost $900,000!

There is actually a double bonus. After 10 years the value of your home will have appreciated to keep up with inflation, and it could well be worth $1,400,000 now if the inflation rate is 4%, an increase of $400,000 over a 10-year period. Appreciation on your property exceeded the interest on your loan by $40,000 ($400,000 – $360,000).

Once the loan is paid off you can use the equity in your home to acquire a property to let, or perhaps invest in stock or your own business. The time value of money relates to interest rates, debt management, and your investment choices. When make decisions around your budget and wealth planning, time is an important consideration. For example, these days many home buyers opt for a 30-year mortgage. Considering that the average age of first-time house buyers in most countries is 36, effectively your last payment will be at age 66. A 30-year home mortgage is a financial trap.

WHERE DO THE FUNDS FOR INVESTMENT COME FROM?

- A lump sum from winning a prize, success in sport, or perhaps an inheritance.
- Employment (also called active income).
- Business operations (portfolio income).
- Assets that generate income (passive income).

The driving force behind investing should be to turn your surplus income into investments that will generate passive income – meaning repeated income without daily labour.

Why is that important? It takes a lot of time, effort, and stress to make extra money. Spending all your earnings or savings irresponsibly means you must make it all over again, and again... eventually you may get tired.

Think of investing in much the same way as geese:

- *Buying geese.* Acquiring assets.
- *Nurturing geese.* Investing in cash flow. Looking after your stock or real estate.
- *Trading geese.* Trading means relying on capital gains. Hoping a 'greater fool' will come along and pay more for the same thing. Trading to win is gambling, not investing.
- *Slaughtering geese:* Selling assets that could have provided consistent income over a long term.

One option to achieve riches is simply to avoid the most common financial mistakes that people make (I know some items were mentioned before):

- Overspending every month or spending without a plan.
- Repeated expenses like TV, takeaways and garden services.
- Living in a much larger that needed house and garden.
- Using the your redraw facility on your home loan like a piggy bank.
- Constantly delaying retirement planning.
- Ignoring the fact that 'luxury' is not necessarily 'last longer' or 'better quality'.

- Co-signing a loan.
- Being underinsured or completely ignoring insurance.
- Incurring debt for consumer goods.
- Ignoring the fact that you need skills to budget, invest, and build wealth.
- Day trading and attempting to 'time the market' is taking on an all-or nothing approach, which mostly ends up in nothing-at-all.
- Falling into the 'lifestyle creep' – earn more, spend more.
- Absence of a short- and long-term money plan.

CHAPTER 4

IDEAS TO INCREASE YOUR NET WORTH

Knowing and managing your net worth can be a lifesaver. If your net worth is falling year on year without you being aware of it, you could spiral down into a desperate debt cycle.

Calculate your net worth. It will tell you:

- Are you in the red? This is a call to action.
- You're in the black? A job well done!

Now compare your current status with previous years. The trends are most important. Negative trends (red lights flashing) are a call for a financial plan. A positive trend is an indicator that your wealth-building plan is on track.

Think about it this way. How would you get to the top of the Empire State Building if the lifts were out of order? The answer is simple – step-by-step. Adopt the same step-by-step approach to improve or fix your financial affairs. We must start with the basics:

1. Do the monthly budget. Know what comes in and what goes out.
2. Know your net worth. Estimate your worth three, five and even 10 years ago. Trends will confirm the pace at which your net worth is growing.
3. Consolidate your debt in your home loan. A single account is easier to manage, and home loans offer the lowest interest rates.
4. If there is a hole in your pocket, fix it. It could be the money you need to reduce debt, or perhaps to start your own venture.

Budget and net worth are where you start, and they are a huge step towards learning money skills. Personal finance includes income, spending, protection, saving, and investing. There is no one size fits all when it comes to wealth planning. Having a monthly budget and monitoring your net worth will give you a clear picture of your current standing, or a reference point. A few important things could assist with your money journey:

- Your credit score is important. Having a good credit score will help you obtain loans, and also the best interest rates. A loan to acquire a second property, for example, is 'good debt'.
- Spend less than you earn. Even six-figure earners overspend. Creating wealth is not about how much you earn; it's more about how much you can keep.
- Know the difference between good debt and bad debt. Stay away from bad debt. Every debt contract you sign creates another employer. Taking on debt is spending money you have not yet earned. 'Travel now, pay later' is selling your future labour.

- Debt creates interest, which you have to pay every month. Your home loan, for example, is not 'sign and forget'. It will do no harm to check:
    - Is the product still right for you?
    - Is the interest you're paying at the most competitive rate?
    - Can you make extra payments?
    - Is the interest rate fixed or variable?
- Your long-term plan should also include estate planning. This will include your final wishes with regards to your assets and who you want to administer your estate. Don't forget to keep beneficiaries up to date.
- Ask your trusted accountant and lawyer to assist with tax planning and asset protection.

LET'S START WITH THE BUDGET

The word 'budget' is not meant to be restrictive; it is merely a tool you can use to take control of your spending habits. This is where we take stock of our monthly expenses. Once we know where the money goes every month, we can plan.

- Organise your monthly living expenses. Use an app, a spreadsheet, or a piece of paper. Compare income and expenses (inflow and outflow). Are you overspending? Is there something you can change immediately?
- Identify areas where you overspend. Is there a debt problem? Then opt for a six- or 12-month plan to reduce or consolidate accounts and credit cards.
- Day-to-day spending is often a big contributor to money

problems. Create a separate account for consumer items like clothing and dining out; it will help you to stick to the budget.

- Identify areas where you can save. Don't be shy to renegotiate services such bank charges and your insurance premium.
- Know your weaknesses. Do you spend more when you're hungry, stressed, or bored?
- Choose a balanced lifestyle. Status and social proof are the main reasons why many people live beyond their means.
- Spend what you earn. If there is nothing left for savings you may have to borrow for unexpected expenses. Zero savings also means missing out on the opportunity to earn compound interest.
- Earning more is better than saving more. There is a limit to how much you can cut the budget.

50/20/30 budget rule. US Senator Elizabeth Warren popularised the 50/20/30 budget rule in her book *All Your Worth: The Ultimate Lifetime Money Plan*, co-written with her daughter Amelia Warren Tyagi. The idea is to divide your after-tax income into three groups of spending: 50% on needs, 30% on wants, and 20% on savings.

Allocate 50% for the 'must-have' items: insurance, the mortgage, car lease, and groceries. Wants take up 30%, for non-essential items like tickets for the game, meals out, gym fees and perhaps a new jacket. Last, but not least, 20% is for savings and investments.

Make sure to compare the 50/20/30 budget to your net income (take-home pay). Limiting your living expenses to roughly 50% of your income will ensure that you have enough left over for your savings and fun activities.

I know what you're thinking. How the hell can I save 20% of my monthly income? It may be easier than you think:

- Consider that most households spend between 20% and 60% of net income repaying loans. If all the loans are paid off, there may even be more than 20% left for saving or investing – or both. Initially, the 20% may go towards reducing debt. Reducing debt goes before saving.
- The budget is your spending framework, rather than hoping there will be something left for savings at the end of the month.
- Kill the bills. Stop buying consumer goods with the credit card. Interest and admin fees ensure that you pay more for everything you buy. Pay off the smallest account first, it will motivate you to tackle the next one.
- Ask yourself: How much extra money will I have in my pocket every month if I have zero debt liabilities?
- Life is much better with savings in the bank rather than working to pay off debt. Cash in the bank puts you in control. Now you can move from 'save' to 'save and invest'. You can invest in the stock market or perhaps use your savings to start a business or a side-hustle.
- Interest rates on credit cards is around 20%. It makes sense to reduce debt before we save.

A budget teaches us to balance income and expenses. Good money habits then become routine. Small successes motivate us to do better. The 50/30/20 rule is a helpful tool to reassess monthly spending.

- *Re-examination.* If your rent or mortgage is more than 50% of your take-home pay it may be time look at something more affordable.
- *Ease of reference.* In just a few minutes you can assess if there a balance between obligations, the nice-to-haves, and your savings

portfolio, without getting lost in the numbers.

- *Flexibility.* It is just a guideline, no need to spend exactly 50/20/30. We all have priorities that change over time.
- *Rule of thumb.* If your spending percentages are way out, 50/20/30 is a handy tool for planning, as well as to get spending habits back on track.
- *Balance is always important.* Knowing we can meet obligations and still enjoy life is a good place to be.
- *A budgeting system.* Even the local tennis club must operate like a business. The books will tell the committee if they need to save or perhaps increase membership fees.
- *Fixed and variable costs;* Every budget has fixed costs, for example the home loan, property rates and insurance. We also have monthly variable expenses for groceries, dining out and clothes. We tend to overspend on the variable items. Paying cash or creating a separate account is the best way to keep a tight rein on daily expenses.

Consider having more than one bank account.

- *Main account.* All income is deposited into this account. From this account you pay any creditors, insurance, and health insurance (the monthly fixed costs.) You route money to your other accounts from this account.
- *Sundry account.* For daily living expenses such as groceries and coffee (all the variable expenses).
- *Account for emergencies and periodic expenses.* Servicing vehicles, school fees, holidays, and maintenance items are paid from this account.
- *Savings account.* A savings account can save you a lot of money.

For example, if you can save and buy your car with cash you can negotiate a better price – and in in addition, you will avoid paying interest!

REVIEW YOUR WEALTH PLAN YEAR ON YEAR

Setting goals does not have to be boring. Goals trigger new behaviour and inspire us to develop strategies to achieve results. Focus will give us new direction. Suddenly you are striving for something better rather than wishing for something to happen.

Goals motivate us to achieve a desired result:

- *Be specific.* 'I want to save more' is too vague. Goals must be clear, detailed, and meaningful. Ask yourself what, when, and why?
- *Measure.* Check and compare the numbers. Are you still on track?
- *Make it achievable.* Challenging, but still achievable. Goals will stretch your mind and cause you to think bigger. What must you do, and what do you need to achieve the desired results?
- *Make it relevant.* Goals make you accountable. You're done with all the talking; you are now obligated to act.
- *Set time-bound goals.* Success is always a matter of results achieved within a specific timeframe.
- *Evaluate at regular intervals.* Don't set yourself up for failure. Sometimes you must reset and realign. That's fine, but keep moving towards your goal.

Expand your skills and perspective. Education should be a habit, not a once-off. Without personal growth, advancement in career, business, or investing will not happen. For example, a salesperson who consistently learns new sales techniques will improve their closing rates.

> *There's one investment that supersedes all others: Invest in yourself. Nobody can take away what you've got in yourself, and everybody has potential they haven't used yet. – Warren Buffet.*

Educating yourself enhances your point of view and helps you to keep up with changes and trends. Managing financials and systems and creating a support network require skills and knowledge. Mastering skills take time and effort, but will pay dividends in the end.

> *Formal education will make you a living; self-education will make you a fortune. – Jim Rohn*

Get organised. A clean house shelters a clean mind. An untidy desk, missed appointments, and searching for documents and your keys are all proof of low organisational skills. Organised people practise their problem-solving skills. They are proactive, have to-do list, and they get things done. They also invest in time-savers such as automation and templates.

There are no instant millions. The term 'get rich quick' is used to describe shady investments promising unrealistic rates of return. Examples are:

- *Advance fee scams.* Promise a large sum of money for an upfront payment or deposit.
- *Pump and dump schemes.* Common in cryptocurrencies, where messaging apps persuade insiders to invest in something worthless.

- *Ponzi schemes.* Existing investors are paid with funds from new investors.
- *Pyramid schemes.* Members are paid to recruit new contributors.

Beware of investment opportunities or schemes that:

- require you to recruit people to earn a bonus
- offer a 'once in a lifetime' opportunity with an added sense of urgency
- give vague details about profit-making and profit-sharing
- promise an upfront orientation fee or 'buy-in' for a job
- use exaggerated marketing language like 'become your own boss'
- guaranteed income with no experience or skill required.

For most people, growing a wealth portfolio is a step-by-step process that takes 20 years or longer. That is why the best wealth plan is the one that starts today. The average millionaire does not make risky investments. They put their money into investments with a steady track record of growth over time.

HOW TO SET UP A PERSONAL NET WORTH STATEMENT

Setting up a net worth statement is as easy as creating a simple checklist and doing some basic maths. Remember, you are calculating the cash amount you would have if all your assets were sold.

- List your assets (what you own), estimate the value of each, and add up the total. Include items such as:
    - money in your bank accounts
    - value of your investment accounts

    - vehicles and equipment
    - market value of your home
    - business interests
    - personal possessions such as jewellery, art, and furniture.

- List your liabilities (what you owe) and add up the outstanding balances. Include items such as:
    - principal balance owed on a mortgage
    - balance on car loans
    - credit card balance
    - loans and accounts
    - medical, tax, and legal liabilities.

Subtract the total of your liabilities from the total of your assets and you have the approximate value of your net worth.

A negative net worth will require you to take firm action. Even if your debt seems unmanageable, filing for bankruptcy should be a last resort. A long-term plan is often a better option:

- List your debt, including the balances.
- Next, create a plan, for example, to get rid of the smallest debt first.
- Strike a deal with your creditors. Offer 60% or 70% of what you owe (if you filed for liquidation they would probably get less). Then negotiate a reasonable time to pay off the balance.
- Put the repayment into your budget.
- Consolidate outstanding debt in your home loan. The interest rates are lower, and it is easier to manage a single account.
- Do it yourself. Debt solution companies do not work for free.
- Get rid of your credit card.

- Use a cash card (an account with no overdraft facility).

Set your budget, including the repayments.

CALCULATE YOUR NET WORTH

Now let's have a look at the net worth of the Jones family.

ASSETS – WHAT YOU OWN		LIABILITIES – WHAT YOU OWE	
Fixed	**Real Estate/ Property**	**Fixed**	
Real estate	$700,000	Home mortgage	$240,000
Equity in business	$30,000	2nd Home mortgage	$30,000
Vehicles (cars, trucks, etc.)	$55,000	Bank finance (cars, etc.)	$13,000
Furniture & collectables	$15,000	Bank finance (business)	$12,000
	$800,000		**$295,000**
Current		**Current**	
Cash on hand	$8,000	Credit card	$2,800
Cash investments	$20,000	Accounts	$3,600
Jewellery	$4,000	Unpaid tax	$55,000
	$32,000		**$61,400**
	$832,000		**$356,400**
Net Worth	**$475,600**	**Asset-to-debt-ratio**	**43%**

The statement shows Mr Jones is net worth positive by $475,600. The net worth statement (and the budget) for each person will be unique. You can create your net worth statement and then easily monitor positive and negative trends. Trends are easy to spot when expressed as a ratio or a percentage.

The formula to calculate your debt ratio is:

Debt ratio (%) = Total debt ÷ Total assets

So, for the Jones family, for example:

= $356,400 ÷ $832,000 x 100

= 43%.

Almost half of the Joneses' assets are financed by debt. Once net worth is expressed as a percentage, you can compare your current financial status to previous months or years. For example, if the ratio last year was 40%, and this year it is 43%, it means percentage of debt to assets increased by 3% – a call to action.

DEBT-TO-ASSET RATIO

Debt-to-asset ratio is a strong indicator of financial stability. It is a leverage ratio that measure the percentage of assets financed by creditors.

Debt-to-asset ratio = Total debt ÷ Total assets

or

Debt ratio = (Short-term debt + Long-term debt) ÷ Total assets

Check out your liability (debt) to asset ratio

The debt ratio measures the extent of your financial risk. For households, the debt ratio should not exceed 25%. If your balance sheet shows assets of $200,000 and total debt is $50,000, then 50 ÷ 200 = 0.25 or 25%, meaning that 25% of your assets are funded through debt.

A ratio greater than 1 signifies that liabilities exceed the value of assets, an indication that risk of default on debt (creditors and loans) is high. Avoid investing in a company which is highly leveraged, or lending money to one.

On a personal level, being highly leveraged will certainly put your financial affairs at risk. There is no buffer against a pandemic or a loss of a job.

If you have a business, the debt-to-asset ratio will show:

- how much of company's resources are owned by the shareholders in the form of equity
- how much of company's resources are owned by the creditors in the form of debt.

REMOVE THOSE SELF-IMPOSED HURDLES

Get your mindset in the right place. When people dream about winning the lottery or receiving an inheritance, they are not thinking about building wealth. They are thinking, 'What would it be like to spend a million dollars?' People feel rich when they spend a lot of money.

Because people work hard to earn money, they believe they deserve to spend it, to treat themselves to nice things. The results are always the same. The more you spend, the less money you will have. To grow wealth, you need to adopt an 'invest, rather than spend' mindset. If the mindset is 'spend the million dollars', the riches may soon disappear. Then you must keep on working.

Getting the spend mindset right is easier said than done. Computers calculate and execute accordingly. Humans calculate and do differently. Even the most intelligent among us prefer not to look at the numbers when we eye that nice-to-have thing. Emotions consistently override logic. 'Live within your means' and 'spend within the budget' require a very strong mindset and lots of commitment.

MONEY HAS AN INSIDE AND AN OUTSIDE

Outside is what we see. Fancy cars and a big house. Wow, these people are rich! That is relying on outward appearances for judgement. You are looking at their riches (spending habits), not their net worth. You don't know if their money comes from an inheritance, entrepreneurship or, as in many cases, it's all borrowed money.

Inside is what we don't see. Wealthy people care more about financial security. Their wealth is not for others to see. A big house attracts higher rates, maintenance, and cleaning costs. Three average-size houses can cost the same as a large house in an upmarket suburb. Personally, I would prefer the average house and a consistent income from two properties to let.

People without financial and business skills often trust others for solutions:

- They rely on mass action for an increase.
- They rely on labour laws to keeps their jobs.
- They hope their employers will make them rich.
- They play Lotto every week.
- They hand their savings over to brokers, hoping they will know what to with it.

Financial success (building wealth) is a consistent and consequential process over time. If you are overweight, do you consider a crash diet, or is a healthy way of life a better option?

Potential is not a corporate ladder with 10 steps. Growth, be it personal or financial, is a lifelong experience, and it has no limits. In fact, your true potential is not known. It can only be discovered through a lifetime of commitment and perseverance. Successful people don't work for money; they work to improve their knowledge and skills and to find opportunities to grow and invest. Growth mindset people debate, ask questions, learn from others, and face their problems and deal with them.

A TEST OF A FIXED MINDSET

- My abilities determine everything. (Focus is more on talent than on growing potential).
- If I try hard and fail, it will be a measure of myself.

Investing or starting a business attracts an element of risk. When we fear losing our hard-earned money, we start listening to the wrong voices – 'I wasn't the brightest kid in school', 'Nobody in our family is good in business', 'If I fail, I will look stupid' – and self-doubt starts creeping in.

Perhaps we can change our way of thinking and adopt a growth mindset:

- It's only money, I can make it again.
- My learning experience is more valuable than a few dollars lost.
- The biggest risk is not taking any risk.

- Practice is fertile ground for growing skills and knowledge, and next time I can do it better.

Abilities, combined with hard work, are the building blocks to grow and break through our self-created false ceilings. Once we stretch our talents with commitment and perseverance, we will find that growth has no limits or timeframes. A fixed mindset views effort as making up for shortcomings and therefore tends to prevent that person from reaching their full potential. All we need to do is move out of our comfort zone and look for opportunities to stretch our abilities and build character, such as:

- Finding new projects, interests and hobbies.
- Teaching yourself to investigate the true facts and find solutions for problems, instead of shouting it away or blaming someone else.
- Adopting a learning mindset. A mistake is just an incident, it's not your identity.
- Surrounding yourself with professionals (coaches), so that your way forward is always based on an informed opinion.
- Making a consistent effort to improve and doing better than the day before.
- Being organised. Routines, planning, and systems are the foundation for success and growth.
- Believing that success is a product of learning and practice.

Believe that everyone can learn and expand their abilities and skills.

- Accept that we, our partners, and our environment are not perfect and will give us the space to engage, encourage and learn. We overcome our problems rather than denying or judging.

- Accept that even gifted people have to work hard. A 'growth mind' believes in the power of effort.
- Don't concern yourself with what others think – it gets in the way of what you want to achieve.
- Realise that potential is not a tree, it is a seed.

COMMON MISCONCEPTIONS

By believing that intelligence is fixed, or is an ability you are born with, you consciously distance yourself from growing and reaching your full potential. A challenging environment increases opportunities for learning and improving. Many people dream about finding a treasure throughout their whole lives, and completely fail to realise that the best treasure of all is the one inside you. It is your own true potential and ability to improve. For example, starting your own business is planting yourself in the most fertile ground for personal and financial growth.

When it comes to our hard-earned money, for most people it's better to be safe than sorry. Many people are discouraged by the thought of investing:

- What if you lose your money?
- Many investment schemes underperform.
- Returns are not guaranteed.

It is possible to overcome fear of investing:

- *Own your home.* It's the easiest and safest way to kickstart your investing plan. The best investment plan starts with getting rid of all mortgages, leases, and sundry dept.
- *Diversify.* Think average rate of return. Spreading your money

across many different investment types and regions will mitigate risk.

- *Think long-term.* It's the best way to avoid 'buy high, sell low'.
- *Start small.* It takes time to learn about the stock market and common economic shifts. Knowledge is an essential asset in investing.
- *Don't be shy to negotiate.* The lower the price, the higher the rate of return.
- *Automate your savings.* Switch to a debit order and start reaping the benefit of compound interest. A small amount invested consistently can build wealth over time.
- *The stock market can be daunting.* Start by investing small amounts. Avoid dangerous tactics like day trading, trying to time the market, or buying high-risk investments. Despite its volatility, the stock market remains one of the most effective ways to build wealth over a lifetime.
- *Risk is normal.* Investors seldom lose all their money. Markets fluctuate, but as long as you don't panic and sell at a low, the chance of losing is small.

Short-term stability is key in your long-term plan. If your current financial affairs are in chaos, there will be no space left to accommodate a wealth strategy. Building net worth requires a holistic approach. It involves financial and estate planning, risk management, and end goals. Planning should also consider external factors such as inflation, market volatility, and changing circumstances. Accept that you cannot work forever. Accept that people are living longer after retirement. To account for everything, you need to take everything into account.

CHAPTER 5

INVESTING OPTIONS

You can never save enough to become rich. To get ahead you need compounding interest and asset appreciation. Saving is just storing your money somewhere, while investing means rolling up your sleeves. You don't have to be wealthy to invest, but you do have to invest to become wealthy.

Principal is the original amount borrowed or placed into an investment. Whether you are investing, taking out a mortgage or starting a business, the principal is the foundation for calculation your return on investment (ROI).

It is important that the principal (initial deposit) of your retirement fund will exceed or at least keep up with inflation. That's why we have to think 'invest' rather than 'save'.

HAVE YOU EVER THOUGHT OF BECOMING YOUR OWN INVESTOR?

There are only two sources of income:

- Earnings from active labour. When you stop working, income stops.
- Passive income. Earning interest, rent, or dividends while you sleep.

If the idea of investing intimidates you, consider enrolling in a class on investing basics, or invest through an experienced professional. You can mitigate risk by investing consistently and spreading your money across diverse asset classes. For example:

- **Cash and cash equivalents** represent actual cash on hand and securities that are similar to cash.
- **Fixed income** is an investment that pays a set, periodic amount of interest. Government and corporate bonds are the most common types.
- **Equities or shares in a company.** There are two ways to make money from investing in companies:
    - equity or shares in a company that pays a dividend
    - selling the shares for more than you paid for them.
- **Commodities** are basic goods that can be transformed into other goods and services, for example, precious metals and agricultural products.
- **Alternative asset classes** include real estate, artwork, collectables, private equity, hedge funds, and tangible assets.

There are different terms that describe investments:

- *Assets.* An owned resource expected to increase in value.
- *Holdings.* A collection of assets like stocks or bonds.
- *Portfolio.* All your investments as a group.
- *Asset classes.* A group of stocks or bonds with similar characteristics.

There are four routes you can follow as an investor:

1. *Savings products.* No skills required.
2. *Stocks or real estate.* Investing skills required.
3. *Start a business.* Business, accounting, and technical skills required.
4. *Diversified portfolio.* A combination of business interests, savings, and investing.

MARKET PRODUCTS IN THE STOCK MARKET

'Market products' is the umbrella term for stocks, bonds, and other financial option or instruments. The idea of investing can be quite intimidating. Generally speaking, you should not be using money you will need soon.

Mutual funds give investors the opportunity to invest in a basket of stocks or bonds.

Exchange-traded funds (ETFs) are similar to mutual funds in that they track the performance of a group or basket of stocks, bonds, or commodities. You can invest in lots of securities at once. Much like stocks, buyers and sellers trade ETFs throughout the day. Potential advantages include:

- Adds diversification to your portfolio, so the risk of losing money is reduced.
- No minimum investment required.
- ETFs are generally more tax efficient than some traditional mutual funds.
- Can be bought and sold quickly at a low cost.

Individual stock attaches more risk since as all your eggs are now in one basket. When you chose ownership in a real company, make sure you understand what you are investing in, and commit for the long-term, generally about five years.

Do it yourself. If you are just starting out, consider investing through a trusted broker. You can also make use of investing apps for beginners. Consider companies that are undervalued and have a strong consumer appeal.

Active investment strategies. An investment choice where the investor is regularly involved, for example, flipping houses, or when you control your own stock portfolio rather than working with a financial institution or adviser. Active investment strategies are the best choice for anyone who wants to learn business skills and be hands-on with their finances.

Passive investment strategies. These options include index funds, REITs, and rental properties (typically employing the services of a property management company). Passive investments require little day-to-day involvement, but they do require effort and research to establish. Few investments are totally passive.

Understand your risk tolerance. There is no such thing as the best investment for everyone. Some people only invest in stock or cryptocurrency. I prefer real estate; the returns are lower, but it's safe. Warren Buffett said the following about patience in investing: 'The stock market is designed to transfer money from the active to the patient.' It means that many beginner investors will lose money because they're too impatient or because they're looking to make a quick buck from investing.

Day trading. High risk is associated with high reward (or loss). Day trading involves buying and selling securities within the same day. Unless you have a deep understanding of the markets, speculative trading is not recommended.

High-risk investments. Playing the stock market and investing in startup companies are examples of a high-risk strategy.

Low-risk investments. A lower return without jeopardising the initial (principal) investment. Safeguard your investment by diversifying, purchase bonds, or consider long-term savings accounts.

It is crucial to familiarise yourself with the basics of investment options. Lack of skills is the biggest risk.

INVESTING IN STOCK (ALSO CALLED EQUITY)

Never invest in stock. Invest in a company you know and in an industry that you understand. When you own a share, you own a portion of that company. As a shareholder, you are entitled to dividends. The cost of one share is called the share price. The price per share is determined by supply and demand at a point in time. Growth in your company's market share will increase the value of your equity. A profitable company will increase the demand for its shares. More willing buyers than sellers will increase the share price. When buyers and sellers are in equilibrium, the price will become stable, or drop. Education and experience will help you predict future directions of activities more accurately.

Understand your risk tolerance. It is advisable to attend investment courses. Study the stock market. Company financial statements are available on the internet. Is the company profitable, growing, undervalued or overvalued? Parting with your money should be based on educated decisions rather than the 'hot tip' at the coffee machine. Read the newspapers; economic and political events influence share prices. Perceptions and emotions also drive value.

Risk means that the value of your shares can fall. If you panic when the share price drops, you may be selling at the bottom of the curve. Ride the curves, longer investment terms of five to seven years will also reduce risk. Time, not timing, is the safer option. Invest with disposable income. Borrowing to invest in the stock market is not recommended.

You can choose your level of exposure to risk. Money market accounts and funds attracts lower risk, while high-risk stocks include derivatives (options, futures, and swap). Diversify to reduce risk. Don't put all your eggs in one basket – rather, choose a basket of shares. There are a variety of sectors, companies, and investment products to choose from.

Mutual funds and ETFs allow you to diversify and invest in many different stocks. The returns are lower, but so is the risk. ETFs attract little commission, since they are not overseen by a manager.

You need both information and an investment strategy (a trading plan):

- What level of risk are you prepared to accept?
- How much time can you devote to your portfolio each day?
- Investing in one company or a small number of companies will increase exposure to risk.
- Reinvesting your dividends will compound the growth of your investment.
- Are you investing (long-term) or trading (buy and sell), or perhaps both?
- Trading attracts more risk and requires more skills to generate returns.
- Don't dump a huge lump sum into a fund. Drip-feeding is a good strategy to observe risk and timing.
- Gambling is a game of chance, but trading is a game skill and knowledge.

Understand some key terms

- Real estate investment trust (REIT) – 75% of assets must be income-producing real estate.
- Stocks (shares) – Represent an ownership interest in a corporation. Stocks appreciate and pay dividends to the owners.
- Bonds – A form of long-term debt in which the issuing corporation promises to pay the principal amount at a specific date. Bonds pay interest to bond holders.
- Bull market – Prices are expected to rise.
- Bear market – Prices are expected to fall.
- Limited order – An instruction to execute (buy) at a specific price or better.

- Market order – An instruction to execute (sell) immediately at current market price.
- Market capitalisation ('market cap') – The total value of all a company's shares. It represents a company's overall value.
- Day order – An order to buy or sell a security that automatically expires if not executed on the day the order was placed.
- Return on equity – Net income as a percentage of average common stockholders' equity. For example, a company has net income of $30,000 and average common stockholders' equity of $110,000. The company's rate of return on common stock equity equals 0.27 or 27% (income a company generates relative to the amount invested by stockholders). This is a useful tool to compare profitability of firms in the same industry.
- Dividend – Money divided among the shareholders of a company from net income (profits) or from reserves (retained earnings).
- Moving average – The average price per share of a company over a specific period.
- Blue-chip shares – Large, well-established, and financially sound companies that have operated for many years. Blue-chip investments ensure capital growth with lower risk and offer stable dividend payments.
- Volatility – The pace that stock moves up or down. A lower volatility means that a security's value tends to be steady.
- Liquidity – How easily can you sell your stock?
- Forex – Trading in different currencies.
- Broker – The person who buys and sells on your behalf in exchange for a fee.

Stock offers golden opportunities to hedge against inflation:

- Gold. Often viewed an alternative currency, gold is seen as a standard of measurement. It stores value, holding its worth over time. In times of crisis, many investors turn to gold to protect their principal.
- Commodities. Investors use commodities as a predictor of inflation. When prices for commodities rise, the price for products will follow. Commodities include grain, precious metals, electricity, oil, and cattle.
- A 60/40 stock/bond portfolio. A 60/40 stock/bond portfolio is considered to be a well-balanced portfolio. The strategy is a traditional mix of stocks (60%) and bonds (40%).

INVESTING IN A BUSINESS

Not all business ideas require the same ingredients. Some businesses can be owner-managed, others may need staff or have high set-up costs. You can choose to start from scratch, or perhaps you could look at buying a going concern. Partnerships offer the advantage of shared risk and expertise.

Do you have an idea for a business? It should fit you budget and skills.

Is there a demand for your product? Creating awareness for a new product or service requires expensive marketing strategies. Existing ideas are easier to sell.

Competitive advantage. Customers compare value. In most cases, you have to work backwards from selling price to see if your business plan is viable.

Scalability. If there are no possibilities for growth, for example, as a dog walker, you will end up working for yourself.

Customer base. Purchasing an existing enterprise will include the customer base, but make sure those customers don't leave with the previous owner.

Low barriers to entry. Expect fierce competition for businesses that need less specialised skills, fewer regulations, and minimal set-up costs.

The startup. A product or idea is only as good as the business model and plan.

The make-it-work. You need operational, financial, and marketing skills. Startup and make-it-work require different skills.

How long to make it work. I changed from factory owner to work from home. Managing my property portfolio and writing books required no startup time. My coaching business took 12 months to take off. The list for home-based businesses is endless. How long will it take for your idea to become feasible? It all depends on the type of business you choose, customer demand, and your ability to market and brand yourself.

What about a side-hustle? If you need extra cash, part-time work like tutoring or selling homemade creations may be a better option than taking on a second job. Before long, you may be working full time on your side-hustle.

Before you buy an existing venture, realise that there are only two types of businesses:

1. Businesses that **can** operate with little input from the owner – buying an asset.
2. Businesses that **cannot** operate without the owner – buying self-employment.

Read more about an own business in Chapter 7.

INVEST IN DIY (DO-IT-YOURSELF)

There are two types of investing:

1. The 'manage it for me' approach. You trust someone else (a broker or the bank) to look after your savings.
2. The 'do-it-yourself' or DIY approach, learning and applying your skills.

DIY options include collectables, your own business, real estate, stock, blogs, and many more. When you take the decision to build your own nest egg, you are also deciding to accept responsibility and be willing to learn. Set yourself up for success by developing your own skills and knowledge.

Own investing often creates a domino effect. In real estate, the loan for the second property is paid by the first tenant. The loan of the third property is paid off in half the time, by tenants 1 and 2. In addition, paid-off properties provide collateral to acquire funds for new acquisitions. Own investing builds both net worth and business skills.

SPECULATING VS INVESTING

The main difference between investing and speculating (day trading) is risk. Speculating is also associated with gambling or trying to make money quickly.

Speculators make educated decisions on the direction of stock. Profits are not guaranteed and don't always realise. Expectations of growth often lead to an increase in trading volumes, leading to a bubble, such as the dotcom bubble of the late 1990s to early 2000s.

If you choose to speculate, research first, speculate second.

Speculators use many types of trades, such as future contracts, and strategies, such as stop-loss orders. However, the focus of investing should be to grow your net worth, not a one-time profit. For the average investor (that's you and me), I would recommend:

- work with a trusted broker
- diversify
- invest long-term.

Thoughtless financial mistakes: The dotcom bubble is a classic example. When greed steps in, people ignore traditional investment strategies such as comparing the per share earnings ratio before investing in a company.

Did we not experience amazing technological advances in the last few decades? Sophisticated marketing and selling tactics ensure that companies sell and keep on selling (and consumers keep on buying). When it comes to personal finances, we seem to make the same mistakes over and over, as people keep on spending more than they earn.

Sophisticated marketing strategies encourage you not only to spend, but to spend more than you earn. Banks thrive when people overspend. That is because there is a price attached to money, in the form of interest. Let's see how people ruin their net worth:

- *Impatience.* I want that car now. If I can afford the monthly payments, interest and insurance costs, that depreciating asset is mine.
- *Divorce should really be a last option.* Alimony, child support and having your assets cut in half makes divorce a net worth destroyer.
- *Spending more than you earn.* The only way to spend more than you earn is to borrow. You cannot create wealth and pay off debt at the same time.
- *Poor investment choices.* Lack of research and poor negotiating skills often result in buying stock at a high or paying above the market-related price for real estate.
- *Buy and sell.* Day trading or flipping houses is hoping that someone will pay more for the same thing.
- *Redraw facility.* Every withdrawal reduces net worth by the same amount. Withdrawals should only be used to acquire money to generate (appreciating) assets.

If you are splitting matches to save money, ROI will tell it is not worth the effort. ROI can also be used to calculate the return on equity, stock, or even labour. If the total input costs are known, ROI can be used to compare the efficiency of different projects.

Own your home. If you pay off your house over 10 years, you can live there free for the rest of your life. Saving $2,000 in loan or rent payments over 40 years is almost a million dollars in your pocket. Investors look at return on investment. ROI is the make or break:

- The ROI on a savings account is approximately 4%.
- The ROI on stock is approximately 8%.
- The ROI on a residential property is approximately 4.6%, excluding capital gains.
- The ROI on a commercial property is approximately 7.8%, excluding capital gains.

Return on investment: ROI = (net profit ÷ cost of investment) x 100. Also known as ROR, the rate of return. Before parting with your hard-earned cash, ROI will tell you if the opportunity is worthwhile. For example, a new machine costs $100,000 and will generate a net annual return of $20,000, meaning the ROI on the financial investment is 20%. Most spreadsheets have functions to assist with financial calculations.

Do you have anything left at the end of the month? The most important question asked in business is, 'am I making a profit'? Money left over after operations or spending relates to profit or ROI. Return on investment determines the ability of an investment to generate profit. Measuring the gain or loss relative to the amount invested will help us decide if an opportunity is sensible. The return is expressed as a percentage. The higher the percentage, the better.

For example: Peter buys a rare postage stamp for $1,000 and later sells it for $1,300:

- Assets are $1,000 at the beginning of the period.
- Assets are $1,300 at the end of the period.

- ROI = ($1,300 – $1,000) = $300
- ROI = ($300 ÷ $1,000) x 100 = 30% return on investment.
- If the time span was three years, the ROI would be 10% per year.
- In the same way, the formula can calculate the return on company assets:

Net income (after tax) ÷ Total assets invested x 100

SCALE YOUR WEALTH

Income is the flow of money you receive from salary or wages. Wealth can be anything from cash under your mattress, shares, bonds, royalties, and real estate. Net worth expresses wealth as all the real resources under your control. A person whose net income is consistently positive will become increasingly wealthy over the long term.

The measure of wealth is not what you own compared to other people. Wealth is not relative; it is a function of budget and time. If your income from dividends or a pension is enough to cover living expenses after retirement, you have acquired sufficient wealth, provided that you live within your means.

Growing your wealth portfolio in the simplest terms means:

- earn more money
- save more money
- invest consistently.

We all want to earn more. Or, even better, we want more left over in our pockets after all expenses are paid. There are many possibilities for generating more cash:

- *Scale your business.* Look at ways to make operations more profitable.
- *Pay off your debt.* It goes without saying, people who don't pay interest have more cash in their pocket.
- *Save before you buy.* Avoid interest and admin charges, and negotiate a cash discount.
- *Supplement your income.* Fun hobbies like collecting stamps, knitting, and model building can generate extra income.

Scale vs growth. In business, scaling refer to efforts undertaken to make the venture more profitable. This can be done by employing controls to minimise waste, training to improve productivity, or perhaps installing new technologies. Growth or increased turnover can be achieved with marketing, franchising, or expanding the business by opening a second branch.

The same principle can be applied to personal finance. A side hustle, a promotion at work, return on investments are all options to increase income.

BEWARE OF...

- *Financial advisers.* They use your investment to create passive income, earning monthly commission from your investment.
- *Pyramid and Ponzi schemes.* An unsustainable investment pitch that depends on promises of unrealistically high returns from imaginary investments. Promises of big payouts are more than likely a scam.
- *Partnerships.* Easy to put your money into a partnership, but

not always easy to get your money back. Minority shareholding without signing rights means you are nothing more than a glorified worker.

- *Risky business opportunities.* For example, buying a restaurant with your pension savings, but you were never in the food industry.
- *Stock markets.* Investing in companies you know nothing about or investing in a single stock (putting all your eggs in one basket).
- *High-risk investments often offer low levels of liquidity.* You may find it difficult to access your money.
- *Greed over good sense.* Prospects of easy money often overshadow financial prudence.

Investment schemes are often advertised as high-return investments. When stock market returns disappoint, investment scams flourish. Beware of schemes that offer yields over 15% or promise to double your money in the next year. If it sounds too good to be true, it probably is.

Collectors' items require specialist knowledge to guarantee value. People spend years building a stamp collection in the hope that it will be worth millions someday. Most stamp collections are not worth more than their weight in paper. Memorable items with famous signatures are worth nothing if authenticity cannot be proved beyond any doubt. Rare stamps, art, and jewellery have high value, but are often hard to sell.

BUILDING WEALTH STARTS WITH SAVINGS PLAN

Building your wealth can only start with a plan to save. You don't need a high income to build wealth. Saving starts with having something left at the end of the month.

Returns on investment generally range between 3% and 8%. Lifestyle is often more important than interest rates. If you can adopt an affordable lifestyle, living within your means, and can reduce spending by 20% each month, you've beaten all the world's fancy investment plans.

Savings in the bank is the opposite of drowning in debt. Now you are in control. You negotiate cash discounts. Choose where you want to invest. Look out for new opportunities like a new job, or perhaps starting you own business. Save, but also have a savings plan.

'A penny saved is a penny earned.' If you dig a little deeper, you may find that inflation, taxes on interest, bank charges, and commissions charged by financial advisers add up to less than a penny earned.

There are several options for saving:

- You can split matches to save money. You can ride your bicycle to work. In most cases the effort is not worth the return. Being a scrooge or a miser is a loser's strategy.
- You can put your money is the bank, but in real terms, most savings plans hardly keep up with inflation. In addition, interest earned is often subject to tax.

Savings accounts are no more than a piggybank (money under the mattress), unless there is a strategy to turn the savings into an investment plan:

- You're saving to reduce or get rid of debt and paying interest.

- You're spending within the budget.
- You relate spending to your net worth, not 'I can afford it.'
- You're saving to buy a money-generating asset. You could, for instance, leverage your savings to buy a home or invest in the stock market.

Think 'invest' (not 'save'). You need savings to grow your net worth. Wealthy people think 'invest' rather than 'save'. I prefer residential real estate because:

- Houses and units offer relatively low-risk opportunities.
- It's easy to rent out and manage (you can DIY or use a property manager).
- A house to let does not need to be occupied to retain market value. Commercial properties, on the other hand, offer higher returns, but selling value relates to ROI. If there is no tenant, the selling value of a commercial property is lower.

Property may not be for everyone as it requires research before buying, management skills, and a deposit. However, property investments offer:

- *Appreciation.* The value of the asset increases historically, known as capital gains. Even if you use the rental income for living expenses, your principal investment will appreciate. However, it is not advisable to use income from a rental property until the loan is paid off.
- *Reduced risk.* Using other people's money (good debt) to secure your investment. Selling prices are volatile, but the chances of you losing all your money is virtually zero.
- *Icing on the cake (capital gain).* Property is the only investment where the initial investment will appreciate without reinvesting.

- *Passive income.* Once the property is paid off, you can live off the rent income – it's called passive income.
- *Additional income.* A cottage, room or storage space can also be rented out to generate income.

The four most lucrative assets that you can choose from are:

- *Paper.* Items such as stocks, bonds, or mutual funds.
- *Commodities.* Materials like gold and silver.
- *Business.* Invest in a business with the goal of building a sellable entity or a money-generating asset that will generate passive income with minimum input from you.
- *Real estate.* Generate passive income through rental properties and benefit from capital gains when selling a property.

RELY ON CUMULATIVE RESULTS

Albert Einstein said, 'Compound interest is the eighth wonder of the world.'

The cumulative effect can be a positive or a negative spiral. Think of investing as like making a snowball. It takes consistent effort to push the ball until it is so big that it will start rolling by itself. That point where the snowball starts rolling unaided is where your money starts working for you. The snowball effect is caused by growth upon growth, the concept of compound growth.

It yields amazing results:

- If you could fold a piece of paper 42 times it would be thick enough to reach the moon.
- 24 rabbits in Australia became two million in only a decade.

- Put a grain of rice on the first square of a chess board, and two grains on the second square, four on the third... all of the rice in India wouldn't be enough the final square.

How can you benefit from cumulative results?

- lifestyle
- good habits
- investments
- make the budget work, every month
- a long-term financial plan with milestones
- start today.

Simple interest is calculated on the principal, or original amount, of a loan.

Compound interest is calculated on the principal amount and the accumulated interest of previous periods. You are therefore earning interest on interest. Use online calculators to forecast the growth on your investment.

LEVERAGE FOR MAXIMUM ADVANTAGE

Leverage is making use of debt (borrowed funds, or other people's money) to generate income. If the rent from an investment property, such as a second house, surpasses the cost of borrowing, you have made an excellent investment. Your tenant is then buying a house for you.

We use the debt-to-asset (equity) ratio to measure the level of financial leverage. Look separately at business and personal risk. If your portfolio is highly geared, your personal assets may be at risk in the case where you signed collateral for business debt (creditors).

Debt incurred to acquire assets is known as leverage. Leverage is the key to growing wealth, and refers to:

- An investment strategy using borrowed money.
- A strategy to use borrowed money to increase profitability and earning potential.
- The amount of debt used by a firm to finance its assets.

Leverage means that you borrow from others, rather than giving up equity, to make money. You pay back the loan and keep the rest. Leverage increases the ability of your portfolio to grow its turnover. In real estate, leverage is employed when appreciation is highly likely. Funding is the energy to accelerate growth. Leverage is also associated with risk, because lenders always require collateral. Business owners prefer 'debt financing' to 'equity financing' because:

- Interest payments are tax deductible.
- Once loans are paid off, ownership remains intact, whereas equity financing tends to dilute ownership.

YOU CAN ALSO LEVERAGE YOUR IDEAS

Use the knowledge of others through coaching or learning from past mistakes to leverage your decisions and ideas. Actions and choices made today will determine where you stand in the future. Wealthy people leverage their net worth to increase their income streams. You can also leverage your ideas:

- Sequential success (saving every month).

- Compound interest (earn interest on interest).
- Improve every day (practice makes perfect).
- The long-term plan (it starts today).
- Use skills of others (delegating).
- Develop your skills (financial, investing, and business)

RISK SOUNDS LIKE SOMETHING WE MUST AVOID

We measure and manage risk every day. When you choose to drive safely, or swim in shallower waters, you are mitigating risk. Business risks, currency fluctuations, economic turndowns, political instability, age, and many more factors mean that we are surrounded by risk. The relationship between risk and return is a fundamental metric in determining investment strategies. Higher returns are associated with higher risk. Investment risks can be:

- *Equity risks:* Demand and supply ensures that market prices vary all the time.
- *Interest rate risks:* Debt investments like bonds lose value when interest rates go up.
- *Currency risks:* Foreign investments are directly affected by movement in exchange rates.
- *Liquidly risks:* The selling prices of investments such as jewellery and collectables are often lower than expectations. Properties attract capital gains tax.
- *Concentration risk:* Never have all your eggs in one basket.
- *High returns:* Schemes that promise above average returns.
- *Inflation risk:* Inflation reduces the buying power of your investment.

- *Education:* Business operations and market investments require high skills levels to avoid disappointment.
- *Business risks:* Business is associated with high returns and high risk. Business risks include competition, regulations, labour actions, legal disputes, and operational risk.

Diversifying and regular assessment is the most effective way to manage risk.

KNOW WHAT YOU'RE BUYING

The golden rule of investment is never to buy anything if you are not convinced that you will be able to sell it the next day. This is even more important than 'location, location, location'. The ideal is to buy an investment at below market value. To do this, you have to know everything about the product you buy, including the resale value, potential capital growth, income potential, renovation costs, maintenance liabilities, and council and statutory expenses.

When buying property as an investment, location is not always the determining factor:

- The income potential and estimated capital gain will determine the real value of the investment.
- Make sure you buy an asset. If you cannot sell for a profit the next day, you bought a liability.

Investing is the tool for building wealth. But before taking the investment leap:

- Ensure that you understand your risk tolerance. Higher returns are normally associated with more risk.

- Diversify. Avoid reliance on a single option.
- Leverage relates to good debt; we borrow money to acquire assets. Assets produce income and debt on assets reduces our tax liability. Leverage is a process of using other people's money to gain equity.
- Think long-term rather than being a day trader. Value compounded over time increases exponentially.
- Invest in yourself first. Work on your skills and abilities. Know everything about your investment idea.
- In school, mistakes are bad – its pass or fail. Investing is the other way round. Mistakes are good – they're proof that you're trying, learning, and finding solutions. Don't follow the crowd.
- Buying shares in a company is the same as buying part-ownership. Before investing, make sure you understand how the company makes money, its main competitors, and its edge in the market. Is the company over- or undervalued?

The return on investments comes in the form of interest, dividends, or rental income. If you use the income from the investment, only property and shares have the potential to keep up with inflation. Shares, however, have more risk attached.

Work-to-earn pays salaries and wages,
work-to-learn pays dividends.

HOW DO WE DECIDE WHEN WE HAVE ENOUGH?

The pursuit of wealth knows no bounds. When we reach our objectives, it sets a precedent that encourages us to aim for even greater financial success. So what happens next? We continuously shift our targets. As greed takes hold, new undertakings often become less hands-on. A narrow focus on profits can lead us to overlook our employees' wellbeing. For instance, we might hesitate to reprimand our top performer for tardiness, making it challenging to maintain fairness when financial gain takes precedence.

As an example, someone who earns $200,000 annually might envy a person who earns $400,000 a year. They, in turn, may look up to a celebrity, whose earnings reach $6 million. Even when we have sufficient resources, social comparisons can distort our perception, making us feel that what we have is inadequate. Greed relentlessly pushes our goals farther away. This insatiable desire can lead to a kind of gambling mentality, where we risk what we already have for something we don't genuinely require.

ESTABLISH POSITIVE HABITS

Establishing good habits plays a significant role in enhancing our overall wellbeing. Eventually, our behaviours become automatic. However, breaking old habits can be challenging. On the financial front, cultivating good habits can certainly bolster your financial stability. For instance, before making a major purchase, it's wise to request a cooling-off period. It's important to manage impulsive or emotionally driven spending, prioritising quality products over extravagant ones. Always aim to negotiate the best deal before finalising a purchase. Taking care of your belongings makes them last longer and lowers upkeep costs.

WHEN IS THE RIGHT TIME?

Forget about the right time. If you wait for all the lights to be green, you will sit there forever. The economy will never be perfect, legislation will not go away, and unions are there to stay.

The only right time to start your investment plan or your business is right now. A better tomorrow depends on what you do today.

Plans and forecast are never perfect. You make corrections as you go along, and you fiddle with the process to account for what's not perfect. 'Just-right' thinking is just an excuse to delay the start or to procrastinate.

BEFORE YOU INVEST

Pay off your debts first: Interest on debt is generally higher than returns on investment.

Develop your own financial roadmap: Define your goals. What is your risk tolerance?

Consider all the options: Real estate requires more effort. Shares require more skills. Do dummy runs with shares before you part with your cash.

Beware of investment scams: Cross-check banking details before making deposits.

Make sure you can withdraw: Collectables are easy to buy, but often difficult to sell. Withdrawal from a partnership often triggers a dissolution process or hoping that a remaining partner will buy your shares.

Monitor progress: Stay interested. Are you meeting your targets? Monitoring and correcting will keep the investment train on track.

CHAPTER 6

INVESTING IN REAL ESTATE

The three biggest living expenses incurred by households are:

- Housing – 20%
- Food – 17%
- Transport – 15%

The largest portion of consumer spending goes towards housing, either in the form of a mortgage repayment or paying rent. That's why I like bricks and mortar. All people live and work in it. Owned real estate offers passive income, appreciation, tax benefits, ability to use leverage, a relatively small deposit and rent income that keeps up with inflation.

> *Ninety percent of all millionaires become so through owning real estate. More money has been made in real estate than in all industrial investments combined. The wise young man or wage earner of today invests his money in real estate. – Andrew Carnegie*

In this chapter we explore the many opportunities that are available to investors, big and small. Some require no cash layout, for example, renting out space in your home. Real Estate Investment Trusts (REITs) require a small upfront investment. You can choose between buying or building, residential or commercial. Existing properties can be leveraged. Partnerships allow investors to pool money and skills.

RESEARCH BEFORE YOU BUY

There is only one rule in real estate: keep emotions out of it! Sales talk thrives on emotions. Overcome emotions and pressure from agents by doing some research and looking at as many properties as possible. They all offer different locations and features. Buy some time before you sign. A checklist can help you to make a more informed decision. Items to consider are the same for a home or an investment property:

- *Commute time.* Public transport and traffic peak times. Normally houses are not viewed during rush hours.
- *Location.* Proximity to schools, shopping centres and recreation facilities.
- *The neighbourhood.* Bad views, crime, and noise from neighbours or restaurants. What do the surrounding properties look like? Ask the questions. Why are they selling? How long is the property on the market?
- *Think investment.* Consider the future of the neighbourhood. Are there signs that the value will appreciate over the coming years?
- *Compare prices.* Check out selling prices of similar homes in the area.

- *Hidden defects.* Look for sagging paving, state of the roof, cracks or rising damp hidden by a fresh coat of paint.
- *Feel it.* Is the house cold inside? Quality of carpets, doors, and cupboards. Don't be afraid to open and close them. Are the drawers falling apart?
- *Security.* Automated gates, security cameras and security doors can be expensive extras. Being next to a park, busy roads, or a street front garage add to security risk.
- *Layout.* Proportions matter, such as a huge entertainment area and cramped bathrooms. Are the dining room and entertainment areas close to the kitchen? Is there adequate storage space for golf clubs, files, suitcases, garden and camping equipment?
- *Furniture.* Will your exiting furniture fit into the new house, especially lounge and dining room furniture? Ask for a floor plan with room dimensions.
- *Upgrades.* Upgrades will be for your account, but painting, repairs, and renovations can often be negotiated to become part of the selling price.
- *Total cost.* Do the numbers! In addition to the price and registration fees, consider the cost of upgrades, moving, and possibly new furniture and appliances.
- *Don't overpay.* Negotiate and check the suburb's median prices. Make your offer subject to a valuation and inspection by your loan provider. There should be a cooling-off period clause in the contract.

You can also have a deal-breaker checklist. This is when decide to you walk away, no deal!

- Pressure to sign.
- No cooling-off period.

- Refusal to include an escape clause for inspections related to quality, damp, termites, and boundaries.
- Refusal to include a suspensive clause, 'subject to finance', or the successful sale of the purchaser's current property before a certain date.
- No approved plans. It is important to compare approved plans to the actual building structure. Outbuildings or rooms added without an approved plan may have to be demolished.
- An as-is clause may protect the seller from being held liable for hidden defects or issues related to the building plans.

RESIDENTIAL PROPERTIES OFFER ATTRACTIVE BUSINESS AND OPPORTUNITIES

Commercial rezoning. Buy a house on a busy street and convert it into a restaurant or doctor's rooms. You will need to submit a rezoning application to the local council, and end up paying higher rates, but the rent for commercial properties is higher than for residential ones.

Residential rezoning. Most local councils support higher density. Subdividing and developing is a proven recipe for success. The land cost is divided into the number of units for sale.

Should you build, or buy an existing property? Construction takes time, but upmarket suburbs and great views command higher selling prices.

A house with a granny flat: Rental income from a granny flat can help to reduce the loan.

A house with storage: Extra space can be rented out to people who need storage for furniture and boats, for example. Be sure to have an indemnity agreement in place.

Student accommodation: Perhaps your property is situated near a collage or a university.

Bed and breakfast: Even I can make breakfast. Many people prefer house accommodation over a hotel room.

Office in your house: Create office space in your home. Drafting, tuition, counselling, business coaching, clothing repairs can all be done from home – the list is endless.

REAL ESTATE OFFERS A VARIETY OF BUSINESS OPPORTUNITIES

What skills do you have?

- flipping houses or hold-and-sell
- build (or buy) to rent or sell for a profit
- project management, managing building projects for a fee
- estate agent
- property maintenance services
- property management services
- property valuation services
- architectural and drafting services
- cleaning and gardening services
- interior decorating

- building services like painting, guttering, plumbing, irrigation, and many more.

Flipping houses: Flippers buy properties, make noticeable improvements to increase their value, and then sell for a profit. A run-down house in an upmarket area provides an ideal opportunity to increase value. Location is everything. A deep understanding of selling rates and the costs to renovate is crucial for success. Transaction costs, agents' commissions, and registration costs must all be considered when calculating the feasibility of a project.

There are two primary approaches to flipping a property:

Repair and renovate. With this approach, you buy a property that you think will increase in value after doing repairs and cosmetic upgrades. Ideally, you complete the work as quickly as possible and then sell at a price that exceeds your total investment (including the renovations).

Hold and resell. This type of flipping will most likely only work if an offer to buy at well below current selling prices is accepted. Or perhaps you can identify and buy in a rapidly rising market. Little or no renovation cost is involved, you simply buy it, hold it, and then sell for a profit.

Real estate offers unique features compared to other investment options:

- You can negotiate your investment cost.
- You can invest using other people's money (low investment on your part).

- Landlords use rent income collected from tenants to pay off their bank mortgages.
- The real value of the property and the rent income will keep up with inflation.
- A paid-off property can be rented out, generating monthly passive income.
- Properties can be leveraged to acquire more properties (good debt).
- Real estate provides endless opportunities for wealth creation and asset protection.
- Properties offer a low-risk opportunity to learn business and investment skills.
- You control your wealth, so say goodbye to the rat-race and corporate slavery.

How many properties can you afford to buy? There is no limit to the number of properties you can own. The sky's the limit. Once the loan on the first investment property is reduced, it can be used as collateral to buy a second property. Now you have two tenants reducing the mortgage on the second investment. Imagine how quickly you wipe out the mortgage on your tenth property when you have nine tenants contributing to your portfolio. That is the secret to growing a real estate investment.

ADVANTAGES OF INVESTING IN REAL ESTATE

- *It's yours.* You remain in charge on your investment.
- *Market cycles:* Real estate, especial residential property, is a

low-risk investment and is less volatile than other financial instruments.

- *Inflation hedge.* Investment properties generate rental income, which can be adjusted periodically to keep up with inflation.
- *Mortgage liability.* Rent collected from tenants can be used to pay the mortgage. A fundamental strategy employed by property owners to build equity.
- *Property appreciation.* Historically, real estate appreciates over the long term. Capital appreciation ensures that the principal investment keeps up with inflation. A capital gain is the increase in an asset's value between the time you buy it and the time you sell it.
- *Passive income.* Once the mortgage is paid off, the property will continue to pay a passive income.
- *By comparison.* Real estate has a low or negative correlation with other major asset classes. When stocks are down, real estate is often up.
- *Diversification.* Real estate offers excellent opportunities to diversify an investment portfolio, reducing overall risk. Investors can choose from many different types of properties or asset classes like REITs or real estate mutual funds.
- *Skills.* Owning properties to rent is a great way to learn business and financial skills.
- *Leverage (gearing).* As an investor in property, you have an advantage not available to other stock market options. You can purchase a large property investment needing only portion of the cash; in most cases around 20%. To buy stock, you must pay the full value of the stock at the time you place the order. Once you own the property you can keep it or flip it for a profit,

even though you have only paid a small portion of the purchase price. When your investment generates enough rental income to cover all expenses related to the loan repayment, rates, agent's (management) fees, and maintenance, your property is positively geared.

- *Tangible improvements.* Improvements and renovations will increase the property's value, and rental income can be adjusted proportionally.

The purpose of buying property is to convert income into money-generating assets. The 'make or break' factors are:

- *Use as little of your own money as possible.* If you secure a 100% loan and the rent income covers the loan liability, the return on investment is infinite.
- *Know a bargain when you see it.* For example, a run-down property in an upmarket area.
- *Ideally you should buy at 25% below market value.* This will increase your ROI. Research and negotiate. Check out the property websites. There is information related to the median prices and annual appreciation per suburb. Make offers below market value.
- Your good standing with the bank.

BUYING (OWNING) PROPERTY IS NOT THE ONLY OPTION FOR INVESTING IN REAL ESTATE

Real estate, like any other investment choice, comes with its own benefits and challenges. Real estate offers a variety of investing options:

- rental properties
- REITs
- real estate investment groups.

Investing in Real Estate Investment Trusts (REITs): This is for investors who want exposure to the property market without the large initial capital outlay. REITs are pooled investments that own and manage income-producing real estate. REITs are bought and sold just like stock and have the benefit of being highly liquid. REITs offer investors exposure to real estate through shares listed on a stock exchange.

Like regular dividend-paying stocks, REITs offer opportunities for investors to access dividend-based income and appreciation. REITs invest in a variety of commercial properties such as malls, factories, shopping centres, and office buildings. REIT companies must pay out 75% of their taxable earnings available for distribution to investors as dividends.

How do you go about getting REITs? Research and select REITs either individually or via a REIT mutual fund or exchange-traded fund. Simply open a brokerage account and buy shares through your broker.

Real estate investment groups: If you want to own a rental property but don't want the hands-on management hassles, a real estate investment group may then be an option to consider.

Investment groups are a strategy whereby a group of investors pool their funds to buy, manage, and profit from real estate investments. A company will buy or build a complex or apartments. Investors buy units through the company, thus joining the group. A single investor can own one or multiple units. The company also acts as the property manager, taking care of maintenance and marketing in exchange for a management fee.

Investment groups and partnerships need careful consideration. Building costs and fees are controlled by the company. You should do your due diligence on the group and its investors to see track records, rights, and responsibilities. Investment groups are not regulated by a financial authority with strict rules and standards.

Real estate mutual funds: Real estate mutual funds invest primarily in REITs and real estate operating companies. Investors can invest in a diversified real estate portfolio with a relatively small amount of capital. Mutual funds are flexible. You can move from one fund to another, whereas REITs are buying equity in a single fund.

Real estate funds offer low volatility and are fairly liquid. In addition, they provide a hedge against inflation as values tend to keep up with rising building and land costs. I like REIT funds because value is backed by bricks and mortar, whereas most companies rely mostly on good management to keep value.

REAL ESTATE IS A PROVEN HEDGE AGAINST INFLATION

In Sydney, the price of bread increased by 41% between 2019 and 2025, according to consumer advocacy group Choice. At the May 2026 inflation rate buying power of a dollar will reduce by 20% every five years. Inflation erodes the buying power of cash investments over time.

Now let's have a look at real estate. The performance or returns of REITs like TRTX and PMD is more than 45% over the last 10 years. As the prices of raw materials and labour rise, new properties become more expensive to build. Input cost and demand drives up the price of existing real estate. Well-chosen properties, like beachfront houses, often outperform inflation. **Good location always beats inflation.** Rental income relates directly to the value of a property. If you hold a fixed-rate mortgage, your fixed monthly payments become more affordable as inflation rises. The terms of the lease agreement underpinning the investor's rental income is a key mechanism through which rentals can be adjusted.

THERE ARE MANY WAYS TO INCREASE RETURN ON INVESTMENT

1. *Location.* Invest in areas where the demand for rental properties is high. A residential buy-to-let property that generates rental income that covers all related expenses from day one, including mortgage repayments, is known as a positive cash flow property.
2. *Reduce the investment amount.* Research the market. Know a bargain when you see one. Buy from motivated sellers. The closer the mortgage repayment matches rental income, the higher your ROI.
3. *Wheel and deal.* Negotiate the best price. Make a low offer – nine offers may be declined, but the one that's accepted will generate a high return. Use the bank's money. The less cash out of your pocket, the higher your ROI. You can even negotiate the estate agent's commission. If they want 3%, offer 2%. Why not? You are the one taking the risk! Make the deal work: ask your financial institution to lower their fees on your account. You get what you negotiate!

4. *Own management.* DIY can save you a lot of money. We do all the maintenance, periodic inspections and rent collections ourselves. We even find our own tenants. A bit of your own effort keeps the money in your pocket.
5. *Choose the right tenants.* Do the background checks. Applications should include references and employment details.
6. *Reduce risk.* Always ensure that the tenant signs first. Your signature will finalise the deal. All tenants above age 18 must sign the lease Self-employed tenants require extra verification, which can include tax returns, bank and business statements. A letter from the tenant's accountant can confirm consistent monthly and annual earnings.
7. *Reduce on-site costs.* Conduct regular inspections and do the maintenance. A run-down property is a rent killer.
8. *Discuss garden services.* Most tenants don't like gardening and may be willing to pay an extra amount for regular garden services.
9. *Long-term contracts are better.* Every move triggers commissions, contract fees, and possible damage to property.
10. *Small items make a difference.* Keep your property attractive and pet friendly, and make sure there is enough storage space.
11. *Maximise tax benefits.* Interest, commissions, management and maintenance expenses are real tax benefits.

REALITIES OF REAL ESTATE INVESTING

Your home is not real estate. Buying your home is probably the largest purchase most people will ever make. It is a long-term commitment.

The home that you own and live in fulfils a basic need, and so it is not considered to be real estate. Ownership means possessing something in the sense that nobody can take it away. Is owning property real or an illusion? You will only keep on 'owning' your house as long as you can keep up with the monthly mortgage payments. Only once the last cent is paid will the bank release the title deeds. Taxes and mortgages ensure that you are renting from the bank and the government.

What happens to ownership when you die? Most people confuse ownership with possession, reputation, achievement, and job titles. We constantly compare tangibles and intangibles. Ownership defines our position and ranking. We become slaves to our appetite. The things you own should not own you. Wealthy people realise that ownership is not about owning and accumulating stuff – it is about controlling money-generating assets through companies and trusts. Controlling assets includes risk management, growing your net worth, reducing your tax liabilities, and taking care of your family, even in death.

Financial advisers sell financial products such as mutual and retirement funds. They will never advise you to invest in properties. Real estate does not generate commission for brokers. If you scrutinise your tenants carefully, maintenance and rent collection should not be an issue, and your tenants will look after your investment. Financial advisers also argue that property prices often deflate. Again, this is not a problem. In fact, lower prices create an opportunity to acquire investment properties.

FINANCIAL ASPECTS TO CONSIDER WHEN INVESTING IN PROPERTY

Potential investors need to borrow money from a bank to finance the purchase price of the property. The amount of debt that is required is also called the level of gearing. A high debt-to-equity ratio increases the risk of financial failure should you lose your tenant or when interest rates rise.

Interest paid on real estate loans is tax deductible, making the investment more attractive. However, the focus of a property investment should be to produce passive income, not necessarily to save tax.

Ultimately, you want the property to produce positive cash flow for you. Bear in mind that income and expenses are controlled by others and outside forces. Loan repayments are determined by the bank. Rent is determined by market forces. In most cases, the property owner must subsidise the loan during the first few years.

Holiday homes are not good investments as they stand empty for most of the year, generating expenses and zero income.

What if you lose the tenant? Residential properties offer lower returns, but the risk of your property standing empty for months is low. Our portfolio rents out 36 residential properties and in 15 years we have experienced no losses due vacancies.

Longer leases and higher returns make commercial properties more attractive than residential ones, but there is a real risk of longer vacancy periods. An anchor tenant leaving a shopping centre will have a negative overall impact, including reduced foot traffic and lower rent income. Commercial properties are more susceptible to economic downturns. Shopping centres require periodic upgrades to remain attractive. A strategy to mitigate risk is to diversify among residential and commercial properties. Spread the risk by investing in different types of properties and in different locations.

ARE YOU PREPARED TO MANAGE YOUR INVESTMENT?

Any investment needs to be managed, and property is no exception. If you can't do it yourself, consider using an experienced rental agent to look after your properties. They will deal with all the issues related to finding accredited tenants, dealing with slow payers, maintenance, and tenants' complaints.

WILL THE PROPERTY PRODUCE POSITIVE CASH FLOW?

Prospective property investors need to consider expenses related to management fees, agent's commissions, security expenses, maintenance costs, legal costs, rates, and taxes. The balance is money in your pocket, but only what's left after you have repaid the loan.

CAN YOU SELL THE PROPERTY IF YOU NEED TO?

Never say never. You must have an exit strategy in case you need to get out of the investment. Like any other investment, the most important question to ask is, 'If I buy today, will I be able to sell tomorrow?'

HAVE YOU DONE ALL YOUR RESEARCH?

Upmarket suburbs and properties with great views command high selling prices. In those areas, build-and-sell is often a good choice. Average residential areas offer opportunities related to obtaining business rights, renovate-and-sell or subdivision. Either way, before you commit, check out how much comparable properties are selling for. It is also useful to keep an eye on the trends. Are values going up or falling in that area? Speak to rival agents. Are they having trouble selling properties?

Take care not to overpay. Ask the bank to do a valuation survey before you sign. The report may highlight issues with damp or a sagging roof. How much would it cost to have it fixed? Alternatively, add an escape clause, giving you an option to cancel if the bank's valuation does not match the asking price.

Rental properties can include houses, apartments, storage, health care, warehouses, and factories. As a landlord, you can choose the hands-on option and do the property management yourself, or you can hire a property manager. Hands-on management requires a wide range of skills, from maintaining professional relations with tenants, periodic inspections and all the way up to dealing with legal issues.

COSTS EXCLUDED FROM THE PURCHASE PRICE

The selling price of real estate is not necessarily 'land cost plus building cost'. Selling prices are always market related.

The additional costs you will incur when buying or selling an investment property must be considered. Over a five or ten-year period the add-on costs become less significant, but if you are flipping a house or must sell after a short period, transfer costs and commissions will affect the return on your investment. The real price you will be paying is the sum of the following:

- *Transfer duty.* Also known as stamp duty, this is a tax paid to the state or territory government on the transfer of every property.
- *Loan registration and transfer costs.* The loan registration will be done by a conveyancer or lawyer. The loan allows the bank to take the property away in the event of default.
- *Miscellaneous costs.* Moving costs, new carpets, curtains, blinds and possible remodelling. Don't forget about the costs to repaint, repairs to gutters, paving and the garden. It all adds up!
- *Monthly costs of ownership.* Home and household insurance, rates and taxes, levies, water, energy and mortgage repayments. It may be a good idea to double-check the new budget before you buy.
- *Estate agent's commission.* This will apply when you sell.
- *Capital gains tax.* When selling at a profit. Take this one into account if you are considering flipping houses.
- *The purchase price.* Location, location, location.

DISADVANTAGES OF INVESTING IN REAL ESTATE

- You require a large deposit. In addition, you may be required to use your own home as collateral for the balance of the purchase price.
- You are liable to continue the monthly home loan payments, even if the tenant does not pay.

- Risk of tenants not paying. Evicting tenants can be a costly legal process.
- Problematic tenants can cause unexpected maintenance expenses.
- Periodic expenses like repainting, fixing blinds, servicing garage doors, air conditioning, and the garden.
- Even if you appoint a property management company, you will still have to sign contracts, pay agents' commissions, and make decisions related to rent and maintenance. Income from properties is not entirely passive.
- Not as liquid an investment as, for example, stock. Properties can take a long time to sell.
- You will have to pay capital gains tax when you sell.
- You need third party insurance in case there is a claim for injury.
- A property in a poor location can become a liability. You cannot move a house to a better location.
- Commercial properties tend to have higher vacancy rates.
- Interest rates can take a hike, and it may reduce net earnings.
- Buying and selling real estate attracts high transaction costs and agent's commission. An investment property often requires the owner to subsidise the loan for the first two to three years (negative cash flow).

Research before you buy, and screen prospective tenants. Regular inspections can mitigate most of the risks while you enjoy excellent returns on your real estate investment, including all the tax advantages.

REAL ESTATE MEANS YOU ARE INVESTING IN CAPITAL GAIN AND CASH FLOW

- *Capital gain.* This is your year-on-year appreciation. Rental income is directly related to the estimated selling value of your real estate.
- *Cash flow.* Income less expenses (operating and leasing monthly expenses). It is your income statement.
- *Negatively geared.* Negative gearing happens when rental return is less than monthly expenses. Negative cash flow will reduce taxable income.
- *Positively geared.* All expenses are paid, and you have money in your pocket at the end of the month. Since surplus income is subject to tax, it is a good idea to deposit the projected tax liability (for example, 30% of monthly net income) in a separate savings account.
- *Operating expenses.* Includes insurance, taxes, and maintenance.
- *Leasing expenses.* Includes mortgage repayments, capital improvements, agent's and legal fees.
- *Gearing.* When you borrow money to invest.
- *No deal.* When cash flow projections show that break-even will exceed three years.

RETURN ON INVESTMENT

Returns are expressed as a percentage. We compare income with expenses (capital + fees). Divide the **income generated** by the asset by **your investment** in the asset and then multiply by 100 to convert to a percentage:

- If revenue is $50 and your investment is $1,000, your return is 5%.
- 50 (numerator) ÷ 1,000 (denominator) x 100 = 5%
- If revenue is $100 and your investment is $1,000, your return is 10%:
- $100 (numerator) ÷ 1,000 (denominator) x 100 = 10%
- When you increase the numerator (revenue), the return (ROI) will increase.

If you are shopping for real estate, ROI is a quick calculation to see if the deal is worthwhile. As with any other investments, it is important to keep an eye on what you get out in relation to what you put in. When you are house hunting, ROI is also a handy tool to determine viability. Returns are expressed as a percentage. We compare income with expenses (capital + fees).

Let's compare a cash deal with a financed deal.

Cash deal (gross yield)

First, we calculate the total price:

Purchase price + closing costs + remodelling costs = $500,000 + $15,000 + $5,000

Total price = $520,000 (or total out-of-pocket expense)

Annual yield (rent): $800 x 52 weeks = $41,600

Here we only have two variables. ROI = annual rent ÷ total investment

= (41,600 ÷ 520,000) x 100

ROI, gross yield = 8%

Cash deal (net yield)

Net yield is more accurate as it takes into account real estate taxes, maintenance and the homeowners (strata) fee. For example:

Annual costs: taxes ($2,000) + maintenance ($3,000) + strata ($2,000) + insurance ($400) = $7,400.

Annual (yearly) direct costs = $7,400

Annual net income: $41,600 – $7,400 = $34,200

ROI, net yield = net income ÷ total investment

= ($34,200 ÷ $520,000) x 100

Net yield (cash deal) = 6.6%

Financed deal (net yield)

In this instance, we structure a deal based on an investment loan with a 20% down payment. The amount to finance a loan of $400,000 and bond repayments is approximately $26,300 annually.

Costs

Deposit (20% of $500,000) = $100,000

Mortgage bank charges = $2,400

Closing and remodelling costs (as before) = $20,000

Total out-of-pocket costs = $122,400

Income

Annual rental income = $41,600

Total yearly direct costs (as before) = ($7,400)

Yearly mortgage repayments $26,300

Annual net income: = ($41,600 – $7,400 – $26,300) = $7,900

ROI, net yield = net income ÷ total investment

= ($7,900 ÷ $122,400) x 100

Net yield (financed deal) = 6.4%

It is interesting to note that we can chieve almost the same ROI using borrowed capital (leverage).

Instead of using all my savings to acquire one property, I can use leverage (other people's money) to buy two or three properties.

Closing costs include loan application fees, an appraisal (valuation) fee, inspection fees, transfer taxes, lawyer's fees and title search costs. Lenders Mortgage Insurance may be required in cases where the deposit is less than 20% of the property value.

PROPERTIES CAN BE LEVERAGED

Leverage is your tool to increase the size of the investment and, proportionally, your passive income. Once you have reduced the mortgage on your first property, it can be leveraged to acquire a second property, and so on. Property investment is not about owning property; it is about using good debt (leverage) to increase net worth and passive income.

Properties provide a passive income even when you are not actively working – also called a residual income. By contrast, an 'active income' is an income that stops when you stop working. To generate a passive income, you initially work hard, but then reach a point where you begin to receive a continuous income without having to do any significant work. A passive income is connected to an asset that provides a steady income stream. Passive income sources are not necessarily 100% passive. There will still be responsibilities for maintenance, administration, and tax.

Owning property means you remain in control of your investment portfolio. Real estate delivers returns in three ways – estate appreciation, rent income, and tax savings. Property is low-risk and less volatile compared to the volatile environment of shares and derivatives.

A property company is easy to manage. No need for a fancy office; you can work from home. Maintenance, marketing, and legal issues can all be contracted out, and you need not employ anyone on a full-time basis.

Properties can be registered in a trust. It is a good idea to do that before you start an own business. Your investment is then protected from business risks. Trusts also protect the family against estate taxes in the case of death.

I cannot think of any other investment where you can have someone else paying the monthly instalments and continue to pay once the loan is paid off.

STRATEGIES TO CONSIDER

- Compared to residential investments, commercial properties offer a higher yield. Outgoings are paid by the tenant, and lease periods are longer.
- Once you own a property there are often opportunities to renovate, add on, or subdivide to increase value, income, and appreciation.
- Off-the-plan-sales. Buy land and sell units or find investors before it's built.
- Cash is the highest hurdle in acquiring properties. Some people have skills, some people have cash. Consider partners or joint

ventures. A conservative (or worst-case scenario) feasibility study that shows promising returns creates an incentive to invest.

- Offer less. If they want $1 million, offer $800 000.
- Start small, think big. Your first acquisition may be small, but it is your stepping stone (collateral) to acquire your next investment.
- Make your profit at the start. A feasibility study compares estimated total cost with estimated selling rates. What I'm really saying is do the numbers **before** you commit!
- Know your target market. Families want two bathrooms. The toilet for the second bathroom must be separate. Older people prefer one level.
- Add value: Renovate, subdivide or rezone. Converting a corner house into doctor's rooms generates higher rent income and higher selling value.
- Create value. Staging should be neat and tidy. Choose the right agent, and a professional photographer. Create emotion. 'Picture yourself sitting on the deck, taking in the sea breeze', rather than 'three bed, two bath'.
- Set goals. Believe me, it works. My first rented property opened my eyes to passive income. It inspired me to set timelines for the purchase of my next property, and the next one, and the next.
- To start with, don't buy the most expensive property you can afford. Leave room to add value or reduce the loan. This will accelerate your ability to build equity.
- Don't feel pressured. You won't find cool-down periods and escape clauses in the agent's contract. Invest a small amount in a lawyer before you sign. Your lawyer will ensure that you don't end up paying agent's commission even if the deal falls through.
- Find out why people buy and sell. Then you can offer what

people want to buy rather than what you want to sell.
- Have a safety net. More skills and less emotions. Do the numbers and avoid painting yourself into the urgent-sell corner.
- Renovate-and-sell requires strict timeframes, cost management, and quality control. Register a company to buy-and-sell your real estate. Loan exit fees, capital gains tax, and potential investors are easier to manage through a company set-up rather than as a personal asset.
- Be careful of low-pitched or flat roofs: Waterproofing, drainage and flashings need constant maintenance. Low-pitched roofs often allow limited access to plumbing, electrical and air conditioning services. Heat transfer through flat concrete roofs needs to be considered.

The only difference between a rich person and a poor person is how they use their time. – Robert Kiyosaki

WHY AN ESCAPE CLAUSE MATTERS

Buying your home is a major life decision and a significant financial commitment. Buyers must realise that the sales contract presented to them by the friendly salesperson is complex and has been constructed over many years. In addition, there is always conflict of interest. The agent wants commission, the buyer wants a home (investment), and the seller wants capital gains. Real estate sales contracts often include or exclude:

- Sole agency and lock-in clauses. Contracts often contain tie-in clauses and notice periods, but agents often take a 'list it and leave it approach'. Sole mandates should also include an undertaking or agents' performance clause.

- The agent's commission is usually a percentage of the selling price, ask the question; Does the agent's fee include GST?
- Ready, willing and able purchaser clauses mean that if someone is ready, willing and able to purchase your property the agent's commission is due, even if an exchange of contracts doesn't happen.
- Hidden fees include contract fees, penalties, and marketing fees.
- No cooling-off period.

Before you sign, ask a real estate lawyer to align the interests of all parties. An escape clause allows the buyer to back out if the terms of the clause are not met, without a penalty. For example:

- *Subject to the bank's valuation.* Where the selling price turns out to be higher than the valuation.
- *Essential documents.* Where the seller is not able to provide a title deed.
- *Noncompliance.* Where the building on site and the approved building plans do not align, there could be a risk of illegal add-ons.
- *Approved building plans.* In the case where the seller is unable to provide approved council plans.
- *Subject to inspection.* A report by a professional may highlight issues with damp, a sagging roof, or defective paving. How much would cost to have these fixed?
- *Subject to survey.* Possible encroachment by adjacent buildings.
- *What the buyer's eye cannot see.* Older properties may have hidden defects related to plumbing, roof leaks, and pests. The agreement can allow for a 30-day buffer period.

- *Subject to finance.* A finance contingency clause makes the purchase subject to either the buyer or the property or both qualifying for the loan the buyer will need.

1. LOCATION 2. LOCATION 3. LOCATION

You can change a property, but not its location. The potential selling price should be the determining factor when you contemplate buy, build or renovate:

1. *Buying an expensive house in an a less desirable area.* Capital growth will underperform where the value of your investment exceeds the median selling price for that area.
2. *Building on a cheap stand.* While building cost will be more or less the same, the selling value of a house with a sea view could easily be more than double compared to a similar sized house built inland.
3. *Renovating.* Over-capitalisation happens when the cost of renovation exceeds appreciation.

You cannot change your destination overnight, but you can change your direction overnight. – Jim Rohn

CONSIDER SETTING UP A FAMILY TRUST

Once you realise that the key to wealth is not to own but to control, you can start organising your portfolio. The more you own, the more you stand to lose. If you have nothing to lose, nothing can be taken away from you. Put your assets beyond the reach of creditors. Your house, investments, and personal belongings should be legally separated from your business activities. You can do this by placing your assets in a trust fund.

It is a myth that trust funds are only for the super-rich. A trust fund involves three parties:

1. *The grantor.* The person who establishes the trust and donates the home, cash, or furniture.
2. *The beneficiary.* The persons who will benefit from the fund.
3. *The trustee.* An independent trustee is appointed to oversee the duties and responsibilities of the trust for the sole benefit of the beneficiaries. The independent trustee could be your accountant, the bank, or a lawyer.

The purpose of starting a business is to make money, certainly not to lose what you already have. A trust fund, being a legal entity, offers indemnity in the case of unexpected liquidation or bankruptcy. Rich people do not own, they control. Move your assets into a family trust at least six months before you start your business. It is illegal to move assets once tour business experiences financial difficulties, because at the point in time of insolvency your assets already belong to the creditors.

A family trust is a shield against estate taxes in the case of death. Each member must have their will in place.

> *Someone is sitting in the shade because someone planted a tree a long time ago.* – Warren Buffet

CHAPTER 7

YOU CAN ALSO HAVE YOUR OWN SUCCESSFUL BUSINESS

I know what you're thinking: *Own business? No way, that's not for me.* Think again. We all have skills, talents, and experience that we can sell. Being in control of your work life is one of the greatest assets you can have, and an own business could well be within your reach. An own business offers independence, flexible work hours, tax benefits, learning opportunities, and financial rewards. Please read on, it's easier than you think!

THINKING ABOUT STARTING YOUR OWN BUSINESS?

A successful business remains the best option to learn financial skills and to build net worth. Business skills can grow an enterprise into an entity that can be sold, or that can generate passive income.

A business relies on six make-or-break items that will take up most of the owner's time and effort:

1. *Turnover.* Think sales, sales, and more sales. Without sales there is no business.
2. *Cash management (cash flow).* When you run out of cash you must borrow, sell, or close down.
3. *Keep your customers.* A secure customer base is an intangible asset. Return customers make daily operations less demanding.
4. *Break-even point.* How many units do you have to sell to break even?
5. *Brand yourself.* That means concentrating on that one thing that you are good at. Show people that you are the real deal.
6. *Systems.* Allow the owner to monitor and correct. Investing in proven systems opens a door to franchise your brand.

BEFORE YOU TAKE THE LEAP, REMOVE PERSONAL RISK

What do we mean by remove personal risk? Fear of losing money, stress, and legal issues keep people from starting their own business. It's true, business does attract an element of risk. Suppliers seek personal liability. Collateral can include real estate and property such as cars, stocks, bonds, jewellery, and even intellectual property. But that should not deter you from starting your business. All you must do is move ownership to a trust or family member before taking the leap. It is your right to protect yourself and your family against business risks. A trust will shelter personal assets from creditors.

DON'T LET SELF-IMPOSED HURDLES DISTRACT YOU FROM STARTING YOUR OWN BUSINESS

Lack of funds, experience, and long working hours may all look like too much to handle. What about fear of failure, competition, and overwhelming responsibilities? Overthinking becomes a high hurdle. All businesses experience the same challenges. Rest assured, the answers are already there. Books, friends, family, coaches, mentors, bookkeepers, and suppliers have all the answers, and they are all around you. The only questions you should ask yourself are:

- Where does my experience lie?
- What is my passion?
- How can I help others?

BE READY WHEN OPPORTUNITY KNOCKS

You will only catch a fish if your hook is in the water. That means you must set yourself up for success. If you are working for an electrical company, learning the technical skills may get you a better job, but it may not be enough to allow you to start out on your own.

Workers, managers, and owners require different skills. While working, make time to study business skills. Owners have to manage staff, operations, cash flow, and assets. Return customers will be your greatest asset. Loyal customers become advocates for your business. Small- and medium-sized businesses rely on word-of-mouth to boost their brand and credibility.

WHAT CAN AN OWN BUSINESS DO FOR YOU?

- *Your time is your own.* This is the thing I love most about having my own business. Yes, I do tend to work long hours. But it is what I enjoy doing. What's more, I work whenever I want to. Managing your own time is, for me, the greatest advantage of an own business.
- *Your boss will never make you rich.* Successful business owners employ people to do it for them. They can delegate tasks and hold people accountable. Growth in business is directly related to the number of employees.
- *Learning experience.* Skills and experience give you a competitive edge. An own business creates numerous opportunities to learn networking, operations, marketing, and financial skills.
- *Be your own CEO.* Ownership generates responsibility. Owners think and do differently. They set goals and make plans to achieve them. Systems, operations, job descriptions, and quality standards must all align to establish brand and generate sales. Ownership is a great motivator. Just like an owner 'owns' their business, a machine operator can 'own' his/her machine.
- *Chart your own destiny.* Entrepreneurs are in control of their working lives. Business owners design their own work–life balance, make decisions related to growth, financials, and ultimately when they want to retire.
- *Build equity.* Employment only pays a salary. A business will also pay your salary, but in addition, as your business grows, value (equity) grows.
- *Net worth.* Your business is part of your wealth portfolio. As

equity in your venture grows, the value of your net worth will increase in the same proportion.
- *Opportunities.* There may be opportunities to involve or employ family members. Growth can also include new branches or franchising.
- *Premises.* Some businesses, such as manufacturing, offer ideal opportunities to invest in real estate. Instead of renting you can buy your own premises and become your own best tenant.

If I can do it, you can do it. Starting from scratch and building a successful company is a most rewarding experience.

START ON YOUR OWN, BUT IMPROVE YOUR CHANCES FOR SUCCESS

Start small with something you know. If you don't have a particular skill, you may have to settle for a long-term plan. It may be a good idea to find work at an existing business and use the opportunity there to learn the trade, skills, and techniques. Many businesses are started in this way. No need to rush into a business venture. Take the time to:

- Reduce personal risk and liability. Move your assets to a family trust.
- Keep loans and financing needs to a minimum.
- Establish relations with future customers.
- Acquire technical skills at the place where you work.
- Acquire business skills by reading books.
- Acquire bookkeeping skills by doing a short course.

- Be careful not to risk all your cash. Buying an existing business or a franchise business requires a lot of cash up front. If the business fails, all the money is lost and you are on your own.
- New inventions and ideas are difficult to launch. Creating awareness and demand for new products or inventions is difficult and costly. Everybody knows what a plumber is.
- Get all your stationery, letterheads and company website in place.
- Use an intellectual property lawyer to protect your intellectual property rights – such as your trade name, company name, and logo.
- While still working (and while you have time):
    - Find out if there is a demand for your product or idea.
    - Create your business plan.
    - Set up a marketing plan for your product. It may be possible to identify prospective clients.
    - Identify talented employees and sales gurus.
    - Acquire all the technical skills.
    - Establish relations with suppliers. If they believe in you, they will support you.

SKILLS ARE THE HIGHWAY TO SUCCESS

- *Knowledge.* If technical, managerial, and sales skills are required to ensure success, then it will not do any harm to polish up on those skills.
- *Bookkeeping.* Even when the bookkeeping function is outsourced, the owner will keep track of the debtor's age analysis, cash flow requirements, and break-even sales. In addition, the owner makes

decisions about credit, leverage and pricing. A business owner must be hands-on with:

  - *Monthly variable costs (inventory).* Slow- and fast-moving stock. The cost to produce his product. (The operating margin will reflect the company's cash position.)
  - *Monthly fixed costs.* Repeat costs like telephone, electricity, and salaries.

- *Sales.* Monthly sales required to break even.
- *Profit margins.* Is the cost to produce outpacing revenue gains?
- *Debtors.* Are accounts paid on time? Late payment will increase working capital requirements.
- *Results.* Are we making our targets? Can we track our efficiency? You can only manage it if you can measure it.
- *Read the trends.* Are profits stable? Is the customer base growing? Are working capital requirements increasing or decreasing? What is the relationship between fixed and variable costs? The financial statements will tell the owner what the net profit is. Profit can be taken, invested, or used to reduce loans and other debts. Financial discipline is the narrow road to success.
- *Technical skills.* For most businesses, technical skills are essential to survive and be competitive. The most successful startup will be made by a person who has been working in a specialised field for many years. Those people not only possess the technical skills but are also known by prospective clients. They have all the required experience pertaining to market demand, sourcing of inventory, and industry standards.
- *Business skills.* Business skills can be read and studied, but mostly come with on-the-job experience.
- *Bootstrapping.* This is a process of reinvesting profits to grow the

business. It is the cheapest form of finance and is largely risk-free.

- *Investing skills*. Financial success relies on both business skills and investing skills (earning skills and spending skills). Smart business owners invest profits outside the business in money-generating assets, such as stock or real estate. They buy luxuries from the income generated by assets.
- *Client base.* It is possible to build up a client base while working. In the case of a franchise business, the client base already exists – but for most businesses it can take three to 10 years to establish yourself and be known in the market.
- *Technology.* Without the correct computer and IT set-up, no modern business can be competitive. Quotations, cash flows, reports, and calculations are all done in spreadsheets. Email is preferred to telephone conversations. Supplier, customer, and technical information are available on the internet at the press of a button. Your company website tells the whole world who you are. Networking allows for easy implementation and improvement of operating and control systems. The office network makes basic information such as quotations, supplier rates, and technical information available to everyone. Huge amounts of data can be stored and are easy to access. Online programs make it possible for tax, payroll, and accounting statements to be created in-house. You can make all the right connections through your computer.
- *Digital marketing.* Remember your customers are always online. When your prospect clicks on your website, they are looking for something. Fast, user-friendly information about your product is a lead magnet to create interest. Think of your website as a marketing funnel:

- *Awareness.* Your prospect is a stranger, but they have clicked on your website for a reason.
- *Interest.* Create interest by providing easy access to all the information and details of your product. Have a clear call to action space where your prospect can find assistance, more information, details, samples, or even arrange an appointment.
- *Sale.* Turning your prospect into a paying customer.

THINK ABOUT YOUR PERSONAL ABILITIES

- *To be productive.* Are you organised? How do you deal with problems? Are you systems-orientated? Can you set benchmarks for quality and performance?
- *To manage stress.* A weekly routine will ensure that we do the most important tasks. Focus and do one thing at a time. Avoid multitasking; it is the opposite of focus.
- *To manage money.* If reckless personal spending is putting stress on your business, you may be killing the goose that lays the golden eggs.
- *To manage skills.* Realise that the daily running of a business requires team-building, organising, and marketing skills – which are quite different from the skills required to start a business.

If you want to win a race, you must run it yourself.

BUSINESS OWNERS ARE ALSO ASSET MANAGERS

Financial planning starts with knowing and looking after your assets. Business owners often think of their assets as machines and trucks. Anybody can buy equipment. Successful business owners look at intangibles, such as returning customers, skills, and systems to build value. If you are a business owner, or you are planning to start a business, understanding and managing assets is a key factor towards a sustainable business.

Assets are things that must be looked after. If you don't understand what assets are, you cannot look after them. An asset is a resource that has economic value, pays your cash flow, and provides future benefits.

Equity will grow when assets continue to outweigh liabilities. Your asset-to-liability ratio should increase year on year. Detect negative trends as soon as possible to avoid immediate losses – and eventually going out of business.

Examples of assets (items that generate passive income) are:

- cash
- investments
- inventory
- skills and proven systems
- intangible assets (skills, brand, and a secure customer base)
- patents and intellectual property.

The 'return on assets' ratio is an indicator of asset efficiency. Return on assets is expressed as a percentage of net income divided by total assets. Since anyone can own assets, a business should rather rely on intangible assets to differentiate itself from competitors.

Intangible assets: Intangible assets give a company its identity. A solid customer base and being known in the community represents goodwill and is a key ingredient that will secure business value and consistent earning potential over several years.

Reputation, customer loyalty, customer lists, skills, trade secrets, and quality are valuable assets that require hands-on management.

Customers: Because customers cannot be owned, the bookkeeper may not see your customers as an asset. But for the owner, a loyal client secures revenue and profit, which adds value to the business.

Established relationships with clients: Established relationships with customers secures consistent revenue. Understand how your customers add value to your business. Align your marketing strategy and focus on those customers that continually contribute to your success.

Intellectual property (IP): IP is your intellectual invention or design; it is an asset and has value attached to it. IP can be protected through patents, trade names (logos or words), and copyright (intellectual works). Block the competition from using your ideas by registering your intellectual property.

Skills: Employees implement the mission and tactics of the organisation. Knowledge, experience and abilities add value as an intangible asset. Developing those skills and abilities costs money, and therefore the firm must have proper contracts in place to protect its know-how.

Systems: Growth companies are systems-orientated. Well-designed processes provide the traction to execute the core processes, delivering quality products and service on time, every time. Employee contracts must include non-disclosure and confidentiality agreements to protect trade secrets. Well-oiled systems are a form of passive income, since the owner is then no longer required to be actively involved in daily money-generating operations.

Bookkeeping: Well-kept books are a financial snapshot of your business. Bookkeeping records are an asset because they reflect the sale value of a firm. Financial records are a useful tool to read trends and to make informed decisions – looking back and looking forward. Accurate record-keeping establishes accountability to gain finance. Cash flow management, debtors paying on time, and reducing debt are fundamental in taking your business to the next level. Often owners say, 'It's not allowed for in the budget', using cash flow constraints as an excuse. Cash flow management is not meant to be restrictive – it's more about planning. Expenses are linked to sales. Poor planning, not cash flow, restricts sales and growth.

The owner themselves: For income-based or owner-managed businesses, the owner is the most valuable asset. From an investment point of view, the owner will focus on consistent profits from operations rather than relying on the sale value of the venture. When the owner–manager retires, little selling value remains.

To create a business with real selling potential, the owner should focus on the intangibles. Brand name, skills, and established systems will grow the ability of the business to operate without the owner. It will transform the owner-based firm into an attractive investment for the owner, or eventually someone else.

Employees: The accountant may view employees as a cost or a liability, but from an operations point of view, employees have the skills and abilities to produce and sell. Business owners should look at the expenses towards salaries and wages as an investment, not a cost. Investments require responsible management to secure future returns. When an employee leaves, their experience and expertise is also lost.

Value price your services: The service you render is your asset. Value price your service, rather than selling by the hour or being cost-based. Emphasise benefits and efficiency rather than basic needs or features.

Most valuable asset of all: Your skills and abilities.

Sell yourself, your most important sale! Believe it or not, you are always selling:

- A business is sales, sales, and more sales.
- Looking for a job, you will have to sell your track record.
- Applying for a loan, your credit record will be crucial.
- Looking for a partner or an investor, that's a tough sell.
- Promotions, ideas, products, and even goals need selling.

Consider your unique value proposition. What do you do best? Who can you best serve? What are your skills and strengths? Tell people who you are and what you do. For example, if you want to be promoted to manager or director you should act, dress, and talk like one. That is selling or promoting yourself.

You don't have to be an extrovert to sell. If you can add value, solve someone's problem, or save them money, you can clinch the deal.

Keeping your promises builds reputation and brand. Practice active listening and body language skills.

Get noticed. Waiting, wishing, and hoping that someone will knock on your door is not selling. If you don't ask, you won't get. If you don't sell, they won't buy.

A BUSINESS CAN BE BOTH AN ASSET AND A LIABILITY

A business is an asset if it can:

- operate with minimum input from you
- generate passive income
- be sold for a lump sum.

A business can be a liability when:

- it has inconsistent sales, and high levels of leverage.
- the owner signs in their personal capacity for debt incurred by the business.
- businesses that cannot operate without the owner cannot be sold.

THE ROAD TO WEALTH IS CALLED EQUITY

The value of net assets in a business represents the owner's share. In a balance sheet, equity is the book value of the shareholders' assets after all the liabilities are deducted. When a company goes bankrupt, the amount left over after creditors are paid is the owner's equity, or owner's share. Buyers are interested in equity because it reflects the financial health of a company.

Book value of equity: The balance sheet equation expresses owners' equity as (total assets minus total liabilities).

Market value of equity: Real value is market value; what someone is prepared to pay for your business. Consider current market forces, agents' commissions, and capital gains tax when you calculate the present value of your assets.

RATIOS: FINANCIAL METRICS (KPIS) REFLECT TRUE PERFORMANCE

Gross profit margin: To measure the percentage of revenue your business retains after subtracting the cost of goods sold. (Total revenue – Cost of goods sold) ÷ Total revenue). A ratio of 40% means that for every $100 of revenue the cost of goods is $40.

Operating profit margin: To measure the profitability of your business operations after subtracting all operating expenses, excluding interest and taxes. (Operating profit ÷ Total revenue x 100). A 15% operating profit equals $15 profit for $100 revenue.

Net profit margin ratio: To measure the percentage of revenue your business retains after subtracting operating expenses, including the cost of goods sold, operating expenses, and taxes. (Net profit ÷ Total revenue x 100).

Return on assets (ROA): To measure the efficiency with which your business uses its assets to generate profit. (Net income ÷ Average total assets x 100). It's up to you to decide what a good return on assets is, but anything below 5% may be a sign of low efficiency.

Quick ratio: Like the current ratio, the quick ratio excludes inventory from the calculation. It measures how well your business can pay short-term obligations. ((Cash + Accounts receivable) ÷ Current liabilities). A ratio less than 1 indicates that the company may not be able to meet current liabilities.

Interest coverage ratio: To measure your business's ability to pay interest expenses on any debt it has incurred. (Earnings before tax (EBIT) ÷ Interest expense), for example ($100 ÷ $20 = 5x). A ratio under 2x and you are moving towards risk of default.

Labour to revenue ratio: To measure the amount of money spent on employees compared to the amount of revenue generated by the workforce. Labour to revenue ratio = (Total cost of labour ÷ Total revenue generated x 100). Depending on your specific industry, 20% may be acceptable. A ratio of 30% may highlight problems related to overstaffing and inefficient processes.

There is an endless list of ratios that can assist business owners in monitoring efficiency and trends. Consider asking your accountant to check the vital signs. Creeping overheads, aged inventory, debt management, and many more all reduce profit margins and eventually create cash flow constraints. Business owners should use ratios to focus on the few things that create value.

Assign accurate values to all your assets. Rely on conservative estimates to arrive at their true value. The true value of equipment and vehicles are often overstated. The debt-to-asset ratio will reflect your financial progress:

Total liabilities ÷ Total assets = Debt-to-asset ratio

INCREASE YOUR INCOME STREAMS

Rich people have multiple income streams. Coaching, seminars, online courses, writing books, photography, and buying and selling rare collectables or real estate are ways to create additional income streams. What are you good at? Sell your skills. Explore new ventures; it will enhance your skills and perhaps offer opportunities to start an own business.

Types of income which you may already have:

- Investment income earned in the form of dividends from stocks owned.
- Earned income for your direct labour.
- Rental income from properties to let.
- Royalty income from music, inventions, or books.
- Capital gains earned from selling assets whose values have appreciated.
- Profits from business activities.
- Interest earned from savings, deposits, or loans.

Diversify your income and investments to reduce risk. It is a proven survival technique and a safe strategy for building wealth.

Financial stability relates to the ability to earn over a long period of time. Government/corporate/pick-and-shovel jobs often force people to retire in their mid-60's. A great investment is to learn a sideline job or hobby while you are working. Most hobbies such as writing, coaching, buying and selling can keep you busy literally until you fall over. I think retirement is not about 'stopping'; it's more about doing something else that you enjoy and that is less stressful.

An own business offers real financial opportunities. It can be sold or use as a cash cow. Owners can explore ways to scale income for example, if you write cookbooks you can add cooking classes, online courses, seminars, and perhaps even a television show. A swim school can add coffee and a nail bar to supplement its income.

HOW MANY STREAMS OF INCOME SHOULD YOU HAVE?

There is no one size fits all. Experts recommend three to 6 income streams. You'll catch more fish with multiple lines in the water. For example:

- *Active income.* When you do work and are paid for that work. When work stops, income stops.
- *A side hustle.* For example coaching or tuition.
- *Rental income.* Passive income from real estate. Investors can now benefit from crowdfunding platforms.
- *Business income.* Can be active or passive. A website can generate passive income, but most small businesses require hands-on management.
- *Capital gains.* You earn capital gains from the sale of investments.
- *Interest.* Interest can come from your interest-bearing deposit

accounts (savings account), or from loans, made either to individuals (peer-to-peer lending or private notes) or companies (bonds, notes). Dividends are payments from investments and partnerships.
- *Passive income.* Consistent monthly or annual income from money-generating assets.
- *Cash cow.* This is a metaphor for a dairy cow that produces milk every day of its life and requires little to no looking after. The same principle applies to a business that can operate without the owner and can pay dividends year on year.
- *Royalty income.* Passive income from royalties from music or books.

THINK LIKE A BUSINESS OWNER

The best way to kickstart your financial future is to think business. Managing a successful business is all about ownership and accepting responsibility.

- You determine your own outcomes.
- You don't blame someone else.
- You are okay with mistakes; that's how you learn.
- You focus on the things you can control.
- A rigid tree breaks in a storm, so rather be bamboo that sways with the winds of change. Change is good; it keeps you on your toes.
- You don't hold grudges; you appease your mind and move on.
- Business owners say, 'I'm the one that make it happen'.
- Business owners always work towards results.

- Business owners are experts at managing their cash flow, they know their break-even and they concentrate on the money-generating activities.
- Sell skills, not hours.

These things make a business resilient:

- *Cash flow.* There must be enough money (disposable income) to pay for current (monthly) expenses.
- *Overheads (monthly fixed cost).* If you don't watch and manage monthly costs, they just go up and up (creeping overheads).
- *One point of failure.* Relying on one customer or a single product.
- *Systems.* Job descriptions and step-by-step procedures automate operations, create good habits and routines, and instil accountability.
- *It's my fault.* Blaming someone else will not fix the problem.

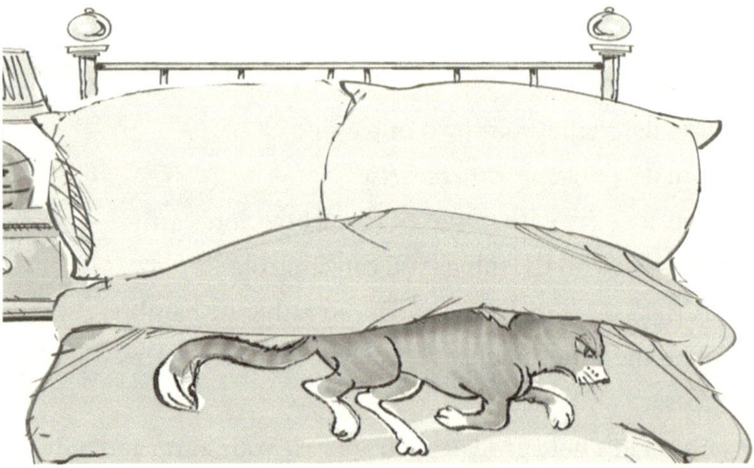

I'm not sure what you mean by 'I'm not taking responsibility?'

BRAND YOURSELF

When a child is born the parents will weigh and measure the baby.

But how will they make sure their baby is counted?

To be counted or noticed you must brand yourself. Branding yourself means that you become known for the specific skill that you possess. The idea is to create a public identity for a target audience. Branding yourself plays a key role in building your career or business. Not what you say, but what you do will tell people you are the real deal. When you deliver on time, every time it shows who you are, what you stand for, and how you are different from your competitors. When customers trust you, they will use you again. And they will also refer you to others. Return customers and word-of-mouth referrals are assets. They are also a form of passive income.

When you work for or sell to someone for the **first** time, you can make sure it is not the **last** time by offering a valuable service.

WHAT MAKES THE RICH RICHER?

Rich people have business skills. They don't follow the herd or those standard sacred cows of financial advice. Rich people:

- focus on success rather than money
- rely on returns on effort rather than returns on savings
- think 'invest' rather than save or spend
- rely on compound interest and appreciation
- use leverage to scale their wealth
- avoid high-risk investments
- have strong networks
- delegate and don't waste time trying to do everything themselves.

IT'S ALL ABOUT RESULTS

People don't want to buy a quarter-inch drill, they want a quarter-inch hole. – Theodore Levitt

All great tennis players have fancy shots. But the players who will be remembered are those who raised the cup. Results or success are all about achieving your goals:

- In sport the best result is winning.
- In business the best result is profit.
- In investing the best result is passive income.

Successful people never attempt success alone. Sports heroes are surrounded by coaches and mentors. Business owners surround themselves with skilled people. There are only two options for a dentist working on his/her own to make more money: they can choose to swing the pick either longer or faster. A smarter strategy may be sharing the premises with other dentists and technicians who can then contribute to the rent and monthly overheads. We can achieve better results working smarter, not harder.

BUSINESS OPPORTUNITIES THAT MAY BE OUT THERE FOR YOU

Many people dream of an own business. Reflect on your skills. What are you good at? What valuable experience do you have? Can you solve other people's problems? Can you save someone money? A good starting point will be:

- Are you an academic?

    - write a book
    - coaching services (consulting, tuition, schooling, training)
    - bookkeeping and tax services (can be done online)
    - online or part-time teaching
- Do you like to work with your hands?
    - building trades like painting or wallpaper hanging
    - repairs to gutters, fences, and gates
    - model building and repairs
    - garden and landscaping
    - cleaning services
    - furniture upholstery and restoration
    - garage organising
- Do you have good people skills?
    - marketing and promotions
    - selling stuff part-time, for example, educational programs
    - online selling, for example, clothes or pizza ovens
    - estate agent and property management services
- Do you love animals?
    - pet sitting, grooming and dog walking
    - part-time work at an animal shelter
- Any experience in the medical field?
    - sell medical equipment
    - transport medical items like specimens, prescription drugs, and equipment
    - home care services
- Perhaps you're good at organising.
    - weddings
    - functions and event catering
    - corporate events and golf days

- If digital marketing is your thing, consider:
    - website development
    - SEO content marketing
    - social media management
    - pay-per-click advertising
- Hands-on type business can be:
    - owning a food truck for coffee, ice cream or hot dogs
    - private chef or baking for the local home industry
    - bed and breakfast if you have a spare room
    - clothing and shoe repairs
    - house and carpet cleaning
    - graphic design
    - interior decorating and design
    - photography and videography
- Is the gym your second home?
    - fitness classes
    - personal trainer
    - nutritional advising
- Turn your hobby into a business
    - coin and stamp collecting
    - model building
    - woodwork and metal work

The list is endless. You don't need a lot of cash for a startup. Use the profit generated by your business to grow operations. Growth is slow, risk is low, and equity remains entirely in your hands. Bootstrapping is associated with humble beginnings, just like Apple, Starbucks, Amazon, Disney, and many more.

THE GREATEST OPPORTUNITY AN OWN BUSINESS CAN OFFER

An own business offers the opportunity to employ people, either full time or as subcontractors. An owner–manager environment is tough. Few solo people can work, sell, and invoice – let alone scale a business. In the 30 years I owned a glass and aluminium factory, I never built or installed a window myself. Turnover and profit were directly related to the number of employees.

The road to riches is through a reliable team. Accept that others can do it better than you. Nobody can be a technical guru, a bookkeeper, and the best salesperson. The secret is to delegate the job and the responsibility.

Perhaps you are contemplating your own venture, or you have already made the leap in business. Try our business books. Books are cheap but contain a wealth of information.

Consider coaching, visit us at www.abilitybusinesscoaching.co.za. You don't have to learn everything the hard way! Coaching is cheap, but you can thrive and benefit from experienced guidance which will ensure that you set the sails for success and independence.

CHAPTER 8

LET'S TAKE A LOOK AT THE LONG TERM

What happens when you retire? Quite simply, the yield on your investment must now provide. Now ask yourself these two questions:

- Will you be able to maintain your standard of living?
- Will the real value of your investment keep up with inflation?

Here is the key factor: There are only two types of investments:

1. Zero growth on the principal amount, for example, fixed deposits and bonds.
2. Growth on the principal amount and also growth on returns, for example, stock and real estate.

All investments provide returns, but not all investments provide returns as well as growth on the principal amount. Without growth on the principal investment, an inflation rate of 5% will reduce the real value (or buying power) of your savings to almost half over a 10-year period. It is a fact that nowadays people often live another 20 or even 30 years after their retirement. Investments like stock will pay dividends and retain real value year on year.

The table below shows that at 5% inflation, the real value of both the principal investment and the earnings are reduced to almost half over a 10-year period.

	PRINCIPAL INVESTMENT	INTEREST EARNED 5%	REDUCED VALUE AT 5% INFLATION
Year 1	1,000,000	50,000	0%
Year 2	950,000	47,500	5%
Year 3	902,500	45,125	10%
Year 4	857,375	42,869	14%
Year 5	814,506	40,725	19%
Year 6	773,781	38,689	23%
Year 7	735,092	36,755	26%
Year 8	698,337	34,917	30%
Year 9	663,420	33,171	34%
Year 10	630,249	31,512	37%

Financial realities often convince people to start working again six or 12 months after retirement. For most people, starting up again after retirement and having to face the realities of the work environment can be quite stressful.

A COMMON MISCONCEPTION

The most famous excuse for not saving is 'the cost of living is much less after retirement'. Are you going to eat less? I think not. Cost of living tends to remain much the same. People want to maintain the same standard of living after retirement. A general rule of thumb is that you need to save enough to provide you with at least 75% of your current annual income.

Even though the house and car may be paid off:

- rates, water, and utilities will remain as a monthly cost.
- insurance and maintenance on the house and vehicles will remain as a monthly cost.
- the cost of health care is most likely to increase.
- pensioners play golf and tennis, which cost money.
- pensioners like to take long holidays, which costs money.
- cars must be replaced after five or 10 years.
- moving to a retirement village is expensive, not to mention special care or nursing.

Saving and investing is not really an option. It is a necessity. All roads lead to Rome in the Middle Ages. Today, 'All roads lead to retirement.'

THE 4% RULE

The 4% rule is a guideline on how to manage savings after retirement, basically to ensure that your savings will last for approximately 30 years. If you retire with $1 million in your portfolio, you can withdraw $40,000 in the first year. In the second year you will withdraw $40,000 plus inflation. If, for example, inflation in year two is 4%, you can withdraw $41,600. The additional 4% ($1,600) compensates for inflation, ensuring you can maintain the same standard of living.

Administering your retirement savings is a balancing act. Withdraw too much and you will run out of savings. Withdraw too little and you will not get the full benefit of your savings.

The 4% rule is a practical gauge retirees can use to maintain a steady income while preserving a sufficient account balance for future years.

Many factors can influence the safe withdrawal rate, but the 4% rule is certainly a simple rule of thumb instrument to estimate minimum requirements for retirement.

THINK 'NOW'

It wasn't raining when Noah built the ark.
– Howard Ruff

There has been a past. There will be a future. But there is only one here and now. Don't waste the 'now'. As you are reading this, you are at point 'now'. Think 'now':

- The best investment plan is the one that starts now.
- Your future starts now.
- The choices we make now determine future outcomes.
- If you don't enjoy life now, it may not happen in the future.
- Now divides your past and your future.
- Now is the time to leave the worries and resentments of the past behind.

- Planning your future happens now.
- Lessons learned in the past can be applied now.

'Let's see how things work out' is hoping for something to happen. Winners make things happen now. In sport, each shot counts, in business each cent counts, in finance each decision counts. In life every day counts. The day might be long, but the years are short!

COUNT YOUR CHICKENS (KEEP THE SCORE)

I know I'm repeating this one, but if you don't know what you have:

- you cannot look after it
- you cannot work with it.

The only way to improve is to measure. Keeping score gives you an outsiders' view looking in. You cannot read the label when you're inside the bottle:

- What was I worth five years ago?
- What am I worth now?
- What will I be worth in five years' time?
- When I know where I stand financially, I can assess, make adjustments and have a plan going forward.

There is a saying, 'If you're not keeping score, it's only practice'.

Sport teaches us to keep score. It tells you that you are a winner, or perhaps that you need to practise. Results are proof of ability. You can argue with the coach or blame the clubs, but not the scoreboard.

From a young age we learn that the score tells the truth. We score all the time. If you are thinking 6/10 when you walk out of a restaurant, you will probably give that one a miss next time around. Listen to your score. Your score will tell whether your portfolio is growing, or perhaps you need to polish up on your skills.

Ever wondered how a tugboat can push around a ship a hundred times its size? The engine of the ship is switched off. Without a wealth-building plan your financial engine is switched off. Others will then determine where you end up.

Don't delay. Approved retirement funds offer investors tax benefits of up to 27.5% of taxable earnings. When you delay your investment journey, the year-on-year compounded tax benefit is lost. Investors in approved retirement funds can benefit from investing with pre-tax money.

BECOME YOUR OWN LEADER

- Are you following the crowd?
- Do you realise that your boss will never make you rich?
- Are you relying on union action for an increase?
- Are you okay with paying interest every month (making others rich)?
- Are you okay with renting (buying equity for the landlord)?

If that is where you are, you need to change your money mindset. Become money-selfish, stop making others rich. Move from *pay interest* to putting *own interest* first. How do you do that? That is the most important question to answer on your journey towards achieving financial freedom.

And the answer is: Are you paying interest, or are you earning interest?

There it is, that is the secret. Interest is the factor that differentiates where people sit financially; the move from struggling financially towards building wealth. Your long-term plan should be to:

- Stop paying rent and interest.
- Own your home and your car.
- Earn interest on savings, and dividends on investments.
- Save before you buy.
- Think carefully how you buy and before you buy.

Managing your income and savings is not a crash diet, it must become a way of life. Become your own financial manager and secure your own financial future:

- *Step 1.* You have to say, 'I'm responsible, from now on it's hands-on money management'.
- *Step 2.* What does your scoreboard say? Time to do the sums (the budget and your net worth).
- *Step 3.* Set attainable goals. There may not be any immediate way to increase your income, but at least you can control spending. Spend as if you are investing. It can be a lot of fun to grow your wealth. One thing is for sure: nothing will change if you keep on doing the same thing.

- *Step 4.* The trends. This one makes you sit up. Compare your net worth to last year, three years, and five years ago. Even if the news is good, you still need a:
    - short-term plan (the budget, to balance monthly expenses)
    - medium-term plan (for annual periodic expenses)
    - long-term plan (your retirement strategy).

Be yourself; everyone else is already taken. – Oscar Wilde

DEVELOP A MONEY MINDSET

Do what business minds do:

- They have a positive mindset. Negative thoughts are restrictive. Successful people enjoy solving problems and finding solutions.
- They rely on their skills and ability to make money.
- They work on the business, not in the business.
- They build a support network of suppliers and professionals.
- They employ people and rely on team effort.
- They focus on the money-generating departments.
- They rely on routines to get things done.
- They focus (it's the opposite of multi-tasking).
- They do the important things first.

KEEP TRACK OF YOUR NET WORTH

One sheet of paper and a few numbers, and you are facing the sum of your financial life. Assets minus debt (liabilities) is what you are worth today. Net worth is your point of reference, your yardstick going forward.

Your net worth is the most important indicator of wealth:

- Are you getting richer or poorer year on year?
- Do you look rich but your net worth is zero?
- What is the plan if you are worth less than last year?
- If liabilities exceed assets, the red lights should be flashing.

The most basic goals for saving are:

- Maintaining your living standard at retirement.
- Owning your home and car.
- Getting out of debt. Debt servicing is paid from net (after tax) income.
- Savings are for holidays, maintenance, education, and unexpected events (periodic expenses).

Perhaps you just decided to work out your net worth – well done! When you start thinking financially, you will realise that items such as your house and car are not assets. You cannot sell your house to buy food. Items that do not generate income are not assets.

Now think again about your net worth. Items that cannot be sold should not be part of the net worth calculation:

- Items that *cannot* be sold to generate income:
    - Personal assets (your home, car, furniture, etc.). Selling a home to generate income is a clear sign of financial distress.
- Items that can be sold to generate income:
    - Personal assets such as a holiday home, boat, and extra cars.
    - Investment assets such as properties to let, stock and valuable collections.

- An own business (a business that can operate without you can be sold).

Now calculate your worth again, but leave out those items that cannot be sold. If your current situation is:

- In the red (liabilities exceed assets) – You need a financial plan.
- Assets are equal to liabilities – How long can you keep it up?
- In the black – Your wealth plan is on track.

Net worth reveals your financial health. The bottom line is the sum of your past investing and spending choices. If you're in the red, don't worry, we've all been there. Honest numbers will give you a starting or reference point to make some adjustments and making a plan to get your money matters back on track. One should really think of assets as things that can pay for your retirement.

BECOME YOUR OWN FINANCIAL MANAGER

The first step towards taking responsibility is to take stock of your current financial status. You could ask yourself:

- What is the total value of your assets (what you own)?
- What is the total value of debt incurred (what you owe)?
- What is the ratio of debt to assets?
- What percentage of my net income goes towards paying interest?
- Do any of my assets generate passive income?
- Can I compare my current financial status to previous years?

There is also a fourth dimension to growing your net worth. Creating wealth is directly related to the number of people who contribute to your portfolio, such as:

- receiving rent from tenants
- relying on a strong network for advice and insider knowledge
- employing people with technical, manufacturing, and professional skills in business ventures.

Most students who leave the school system cannot do a monthly budget. They do not know that there is 'good debt' and 'bad debt.' Their house, which is supposed to be an asset, becomes a liability because the mortgage is used to pay for cars or living expenses. Know the difference between good debt (leverage to acquire assets) and bad debt (debt for a lifestyle that creates more expenses).

Think assets. When you owe, you are an asset for the bank. When you own, the asset is in your book.

The direction that your money flows (cash flow) will determine your wealth:

- Are you paying rent (liability) or are you receiving rent (asset)?
- Are you paying interest (expense) or are you receiving dividends (income)?
- Are you paying accounts from a salary (own labour) or with income from assets or business (passive income)?

LET'S HAVE A LOOK AT THE LONG TERM

A few examples explain the importance of thinking long-term:

- If your house is paid off within 10 years, you can live there loan- or rent-free for the rest of your life.
- If you are a business owner, your exit strategy should be part of your startup plan. In other words, a strategy explaining how to work 'on the business' instead of 'in the business', thereby creating:
  - a business that can operate with minimum input from the owner.
  - a money-generating asset that provides passive income.
  - an entity that can be sold.

If you want to build wealth in business, you need to strike a balance between short-term results and long-term investments. We are all wired to think short-term. We fall victim to instant gratification because we can't eat next year.

Short-term needs often push long-term goals aside. That's why many people often only start saving for retirement at age 50. Your ability to think long-term is a real key to your financial stability.

TIME AND EFFORT

Time is regarded as a precious asset. We all have the same number of hours each day, yet we don't all have the same amount of money, possessions, and success.

Customers, for example, attach high value to time. Customers will often choose a faster and more efficient option over a cheaper alternative because it will save them time and money.

Are your efforts focused on results? In business, managers are results-driven. Employees, on the other hand, are more effort-driven:

- I work long hours; I deserve more pay.
- Should employees not rather be thinking, 'I am more productive, I deserve more pay'?

Think 'balance' when planning your future. For example, building wealth (saving) but neglecting to have comprehensive insurance simply means that a health setback or accident could wipe out your savings.

The best long-term results can be achieved by spending time and effort in the right proportion. Most people's lives revolve around family, work, cars, house, religion, sport, and hobbies. That perfect balance of time and effort will not be the same for everyone.

UNDERSTAND RISK/REWARD

Risk/reward relates to the expected return on an investment opportunity. Traders choose their bets carefully. When the potential yield for different investments is the same, the one with least risk will be the safest bet. Risk is associated with:

- *Probability.* The reward in winning the lottery is high, but the probability is low.
- *Tolerance for risk.* People experience risk differently. The person who is not afraid of heights may be afraid to invest in the stock market. Personally, I don't like high risk, so investing in real estate works for me. Each person knows their own risk tolerance.

- *Assumption.* Will the price of stock go up or down?
- *Skills.* Inexperienced investors tend to 'hope for the best'.
- *Guarantees.* There is no guarantee that a high-risk investment will yield a high return.

Traders compare maximum risk to target profit. Before you start trading, you must know when to take profits, and where you should put your stop-loss.

Investment scams often promise high returns. Cold-calls, time pressure, and vague business models are warning signs of offers that sound too good to be true.

THE NEGATIVES AND THE POSITIVES

What makes you poor?

- Debt attracts interest, admin fees and penalties.
- Absence of a budget is flying blind with your disposable income.
- Buying more than you need, or things that you don't really need.
- Depreciation. Luxury goods tend to depreciate more in value. That is because they cost double, but don't always offer double the value.
- Debt contracts. Over and above long-term repayment obligations, lending contracts have penalty and default clauses. Lenders often require collateral. A garnishee order (also known as an emoluments attachment order, or EAO for short), by written consent or court judgement, allows money to be deducted from your salary to pay the creditor directly.
- Poor negotiating skills. You pay more for everything.

- Emotional buying. Buying a house without researching selling prices in the area.
- Interest is paid from net (after tax) income.
- Paying rent. There is no estate build-up. (Actually, there is, but only for the landlord.)
- Absence of medium- and long-term estate planning. Time is not on your side.
- Sales talk. Discounts, direct marketing, rewards, samples, events, bundles, loyalty cards – the list goes on. Creative selling techniques attract new and repeat customers. Key product features, price, placement, and marketing strategies all work together to promote and sell.

What makes you rich? The things that create wealth, amazingly, are the same things that make people poor:

- Rich people earn interest, poor people pay interest. That is how the economic scale is balanced.
- Poor people pay rent, rich people earn rent (earning rent builds equity).
- Rich people pay for expenses from passive income, (interest, dividends, royalties, and rent).
- Rich people benefit from compound interest and capital gains.
- Rich people build wealth with only three things. 1. Comprehensive insurance. 2. They make use of good debt. 3. They control their wealth through companies and trusts.
- Rich people have financial, accounting, and business skills. You may ask, 'Where do I get those skills?'
    - Experience from work (practical, hands-on skills are still number one).

  - Learning institutions offer courses in leadership, networking, accounting, project and business management.
  - Colleges and universities.
  - Self-learning. Books, magazines, and videos may not include a certificate to hang on the wall, but they are cheap and easy to come by. Self-learning is a great spare time activity. Business books available on Amazon or in the bookshop around the corner contain all the know-how you need to run a successful business (I wish I knew that when I started my business)!

THIS STEP-BY-STEP GUIDE ENSURES THAT YOU GROW YOUR NET WORTH

- *The mindset.* Realise your earnings need discipline and management.
- *The budget.* I know you won't get it right the first month. Skills take time to learn, but reap huge benefits in the long run.
- *Net worth.* Know your assets and grow your assets.
- *Debt.* Should only be your home loan.
- *Save.* For school fees, emergencies, holidays.
- *Retirement planning.* Could be employer-sponsored, real estate, stock, bonds, or annuity funds. Avoid cashing in. After retirement, consider working longer doing less stressful work-from-home jobs like tutoring or baking to stretch your savings.
- *Your own venture.* Starting my own business proved to be the best decision I ever made. It was never easy, but at least I can retire easily.

USE THE 'BE–DO–HAVE' PRINCIPLE

Start with the 'have.' You want to 'have' more money in your pocket.

What must you 'be' to get the 'have'? Perhaps you will need more financial skills and a bit of discipline. Like a diet, the plan will include a change in lifestyle.

What must you 'do' to get the 'have'? It could be to get rid of the credit card and wipe out all the small debt. In other words, you need to have a *goal* and a *plan* to get the 'have'.

First, your *goal*, then your *plan* for how to get there. Goals must be SMART.

- *Specific.* You want spare money in your pocket to reduce debt on card and accounts.
- *Measurable.* To do that, you decide to save, for example, $500 every month.
- *Attainable.* You checked the numbers and if you stick to the budget, $500 per month is realistic.
- *Timely.* The goal is the wipe out all small debts over the next 12 months.

I can testify that setting goals contributed greatly to building my property portfolio. As soon as new property was rented out, I was already making plans to acquire the next one. A goal and a plan get the mindset in the right place gets you going in the right direction.

LAST THOUGHTS

SEVEN PILLARS THAT WILL SUPPORT YOUR WEALTH PLAN

If you've come this far, well done! I know, it's a lot of information to take in. No worries. Just start off with the seven pillars that create wealth.

1. Your home. Own your home. Since you must live somewhere, you might as well make a loan payment rather than a rent payment each month.

2. Your car. Don't let your car make you poor. An affordable car will also get you there. A paid-off car is an asset, increasing your net worth.

3. Budgeting. This includes a plan to get rid of debt. If you are serious about building your wealth, your only debt should be the mortgage on your house (an appreciating asset).

4. Risk management. Insure your goods and your life. Avoid a single point of failure situation.

5. Retirement. How much do you need to retire? Your financial plan will revolve around that question.

6. Estate planning. Your will says how, when, and to whom your assets are transferred after death. This may include a succession plan for a successful business transfer.

7. Invest in yourself. Successful people reap long-term dividends from investing in self-improvement and education. Before you spend all your time, energy, and money, it is important to recognise that returns are directly linked to making the right investment choices. Developing expertise in your field of choice will set you apart from the competition, constantly improving your odds of success. Experts make their own decisions, rather than listening to sales talk. See yourself as your biggest asset. Work on your skills. Budgeting, reading, and side-hustles are all ways to improve skills and abilities. Before long, you may be managing your own business.

BELIEVE IN THE EFFECT OF COMPOUNDED EFFORT

Time is your friend; impulse is your enemy.
– John C. Bogle

DO YOUR SPECIAL THING TODAY

Today is the first day of the rest of your life. Many successful people confess that their wealth is the result of one or two groundbreaking decisions. My own portfolio took off when I decided to rent out the properties I built, instead of selling them. Your mindset today can change your financial future:

- Life isn't fair, but it's still good.
- When in doubt, just take the baby steps.
- Your job won't take care of you when you are sick. Your friends and family will.
- Don't buy stuff you don't need.
- You don't always have to win every argument. Stay true to yourself.
- It's okay to get angry with God. He can take it.
- Save for things that matter.
- Make peace with your past so it won't screw up the present.
- Don't compare your life to others'. You have no idea what their journey is all about.
- If a relationship must be a secret, you shouldn't be in it.
- Everything can change in the blink of an eye, so be prepared.
- Take a deep breath. It calms the mind.
- When it comes to going after what you love in life, don't take no for an answer.
- Don't save things for a special occasion. Today is special.
- Frame every so-called disaster with these words: 'In five years' time, will this matter?'
- Time heals almost everything. Give time.

- When you're angry, stop, time out (for at least two days), think, discuss, consider options, and regain control.
- However good or bad a situation is, it will change; just keep going.

THREE THINGS TO AVOID

1. *Never become a guarantor for debt.* You could end up with a bad credit record.
2. *Never lend money.* The lender hates you because they have to repay you.
3. *Never give free advice.* If something goes wrong, it will be your fault.

EQ IS MORE IMPORTANT THAN IQ

Book wise is IQ, streetwise is EQ; your emotional intelligence. Pairing book skills with emotional skills will take you to the next level.

Being aware of EQ can improve your ability to make rational decisions. Start off with self-management. Make sure your home and office are neat and organised. Title deeds, certificates, contracts, and your will should be kept safe. Self-awareness is next. Improve those soft skills (mind tools) you need to perceive, control, and evaluate before making important decisions.

Emotional intelligence allows us to respond instead of reacting.

A TRIANGLE IS THE STRONGEST SHAPE

Triangles represent geometric sturdiness, three sides of equal strength. They support bridges, roofs, and even aeroplanes. Boat sails, pyramids and a pizza slice are all triangles. Three equal sides give structure to an idea or principle. On a spiritual level, it could be mind–body–spirit. Think of past–present–future. An athlete needs talent–practice–coaching. Business relies on product–sales–customer for success. Think of your financial future as budget–net worth–passive income. Manage your salary with income–budget–expense.

All things require effort. Being a parent is not child's play. Being a baker is not a piece of cake. Managing your finances is not plain sailing. Responsibility is everywhere. Not all things are perfect, that's why we strive every day to make them better. Working harder or longer is not always the solution. When things are not going as they should, it's time to stop, plan, and set achievable goals to get things back on track.

Everything we have is the result of effort.

A FINAL THOUGHT

When South African swimmer Tatjana Schoenmaker won silver in the Olympics, a journalist made this statement in an interview with her parents: 'You must be disappointed that she did not win.' They answered, 'She may have silver around her neck, but she has gold in her heart.' Tatjana herself said swimming does not define who she is, winning or losing does not define who she is.

When we fail, we can quit or we can try again; that defines who we are. People who choose a modest lifestyle do not show off shiny objects; they wear their gold in their hearts.

You must have a financial plan. Think of your financial affairs as being like a firefighter trying to put out a fire with a leaking bucket. As the hole in the bucket (your debt) gets bigger and bigger, you must start making choices. Do you run faster and faster, or is the long-term solution to stop and fix the hole? You cannot solve money issues by working harder or longer. You need to stop, plan, and put achievable financial goals in place.

Be happy today. Some people believe spending makes you happy. 'Shop until you drop' creates temporary satisfaction. Only problem is, you have to keep on spending to remain happy. Compulsive spending reflects an irresponsible way of life, almost like having a hole in your pocket that you don't bother to fix.

Dreaming about an inheritance or hoping to win the lottery is a subconscious way of sidestepping responsibility. Real value lies in your way of life, the cumulative effect of what we do every day. If happiness is 'when I have enough money', then I'm afraid it might never happen.

Perhaps you wondered about the compass on the front page of this book. A compass is all about direction. All you need to do is set the goals and your compass (money plan) will get you there. Goals reflect our purpose in life; they are the driving force behind everything we do. Goals determine where you are going and where you will end up down the line. Goals inspire discipline and an organized and innovative way of doing things. With a strong enough purpose, the 'how's will take care of themselves.

It doesn't matter where in life you walk, on the beach, the internet, even your financial history leaves tracks. The tracks you leave tell a story of credit and credibility. A sound credit record can be a lifeline. Few people will not require credit at some point in time, and lenders are sure to follow your credibility tracks.

I wish you all the best in building your wealth portfolio. For most people, the road to financial independence is long. Achieving realistic goals is a great motivator to keep moving!

Dream, but dream with your eyes wide open

Before I forget. What does Willie Kruger do these days? I sold my factory and am now semi-retired. I manage my property portfolio and share my knowledge. Please visit my coaching site at www.abilitybusinesscoaching.co.za.

Coaching is very affordable, and it can change your financial life.

Thank you for reading my book.

www.ingramcontent.com/pod-product-compliance
Lightning Source LLC
LaVergne TN
LVHW100309210926
848480LV00003B/1066